ISLAM AND CHRISTIANITY IN INDIA AND THE FAR EAST

ISLAM AND CHRISTIANITY IN INDIA AND THE FAR EAST

BY

ELWOOD MORRIS WHERRY

GYAN

ISBN : 978-81-212-1584-8(HB)

First Published, 1907

Published, 2018

Published by

Gyan Publishing House
5, Ansari Road
Daryaganj, New Delhi-110002
Phone: 011-47034999, 9811692060
www.gyanbooks.com
E-mail: books@gyanbooks.com

Printed at: G. Print Process, Delhi.

To My Co-workers

in

Missions to Moslems

PREFACE

THE Papers published in this volume, prepared specially for the Students' Lecture Course on Missions at the Princeton Theological Seminary, sum up the results of many years of study in connection with missionary work in India. The object has not been so much to present what is most interesting in connection with the cause of missions to Mohammedans, as to set forth the facts and conditions under which, on the one hand, Islam has been propagated in India and the countries farther east, and on the other, Christianity has established its missions for the evangelisation of all non-Christians, Moslems included. In the accomplishment of this purpose I have endeavoured to give a brief account of the religion of Islam, in order to show the character and quality of the work to be done in order to evangelise its votaries. Two chapters are then devoted to an account of the propagation of Islam in India and the Far East.

One of these emphasises the services of the proselyting sword. The other illustrates the power which Islam has exerted along the line of preaching. Taken together, these chapters show that in Islam, preaching and teaching normally follow upon the heels of the invading Moslem army, and on the other hand that the preaching of Islam invariably calls in the aid of the secular power. We also learn how very difficult it is for a Church once made subject to the Moslem conqueror to exert any active influence for the evangelisation of its Moslem neighbours.

In the following chapters I have endeavoured to give an account of the Church's endeavour to bring the Gospel to the Moslems in India, China and Malaysia. This endeavour now appears not unlike the efforts of those intrepid travellers who many years since started out to discover the sources of the Nile. One after another entered upon this most difficult undertaking, each accomplished something of value, but for a long time the intrepid voyager either sacrificed his life in the wilds of Central Africa or returned to confess a failure. In due time the persistence of man has revealed the secret; the sealed doors at the head of the great mysterious river have been opened and once more the deserts of Egypt and Nubia are being converted into fruitful fields. The missionaries of the Eastern and Western Catholic Churches have done their work. Great tomes were written by them to expound to Christian readers the Quran and the Traditions of Islam. Some Moslems were converted, but the light of the Gospel was so obscured by the darkness of superstition and idolatry as to fail to reveal the way to the hearts of the followers of Mohammed. It remained for Protestant Christianity to bring to the Moslems of India and the Far East the clear light of the teachings of Jesus Christ. It remained for Protestant governments to bring to the Moslem world the gospel of religious liberty and to enable the Christian evangelist to present the saving truth of God's Word to his Moslem hearer without let or hindrance.

I have endeavoured to indicate some of the dangers which beset the agents of the Church in their evangelistic work among Moslems. My supreme desire is that the reading of this book may convince every Christian missionary that the weapons which will best bring victory to the Christian standards are prayer for the power of God's Holy Spirit to guide and prompt every word and act for their evangelisation, to enable the Christian to voice the Gospel in his life and dealings with them, and finally to place his dependence upon the Bible as the sword of the Spirit, able to convince and to convert the hearts of Moslem readers and hearers.

God has vouchsafed much success to the work already begun. The Moslem may now read the Gospels in his own mother tongue in any part of the world. Many who once were faithful followers of Islam are now zealous preachers of the Gospel. The Christian schools and colleges are busy educating Moslem youth and a thousand influences are being exerted to show the Mohammedan world the truth as it is in Jesus.

Finally, it has been my hope that the reading of these chapters would impress upon those who have in hand the direction of the work of Missionary societies the great importance of having a number of men, thoroughly qualified by a practical acquaintance with the Arabic language and the literature of Islam, whom they could send into mission fields where Moslems live, with a view to some special work for the conversion of these monotheists to Christianity.

Many such fields are now open to missionary endeavour. For them we need the best men the Church can afford—men who, in the spirit of Henry Martyn, Isidor Loewenthal, Ion Keith Falconer, Bishop French, Peter Zwemer, and many others gone to their reward, hold not their lives dear; men who carry the burden of these millions of Moslems upon their hearts, and with Abraham of old cry out: "O, that Ishmael might live before thee!" The one thing we need to bear in mind is that the Moslem must not be treated as a heathen. They accord us the honourable title of Ahl-i-Kitab, People of the Book, because we believe in a revealed religion. They, too, believe in a revealed religion. Let us take them on their own ground and as those zealous for the Word of God challenge them to stand with us upon this claim that we are the People of the Book. "To the Word and the testimony." Here is the issue, and, standing here in His name who has all power in heaven and earth, who is the only sinless prophet of Islam, who is in heaven where He ever maketh intercession for all who call upon His name, and who shall come again, we need not fear the result.

In the preparation of this book, I have been dependent upon many, whose works I have consulted and from whom I have quoted. A list of these is given elsewhere. To these writers I desire to confess my obligation and in the name of my co-labourers I would thank them for the service they have rendered to the cause of Moslem evangelisation.

ELWOOD MORRIS WHERRY

CONTENTS

I

ISLAM AS A RELIGION

ISLAM, like Christianity, has undergone many changes since it was first promulgated. There is, of course, a system of fundamental doctrine which is everywhere recognised; but, like the human form, this system may undergo so many changes in its outward complexion and habiliments as to make the religion of one sect or race differ materially from that of another. Any traveller in Egypt or Russia would readily recognise a Christian church and its service on the Lord's day, and yet its appointments, the vestments of its ministers and the forms of service, would seem so strange as to make him feel himself to be among strangers. The use of charms, the holy water, the reverence paid to the images and pictures of the saints, and the superstitious ceremonies and attitudes of the worshippers, would possibly make him feel that he was mistaken in supposing that he had entered a place consecrated to the worship of the true God. In like manner such a traveller, if visiting the mosques of the Mussulmans in Egypt or Turkey would find the rites and ceremonies of worship to accord with his ideal as learned from the standard writings on the religion of Islam. But when he should undertake to acquaint himself with Islam as it is practised by villagers in Bengal or those in China and Malaysia, he would often be in doubt as to whether these men, with their charms and their reverence for the tombs and pillars erected in the honour of saints, were really Moslems at all. Not long ago, an American writer, describing the manners, and customs of the natives of the Island of Mindanao, said he could not understand their aversion to pork. And even when one of the natives told him a story to show why it was, he did not apprehend the fact that those people were Mohammedans. So long had these poor people been without the usual teachings of the mullahs, so long had they concealed their identity from their Spanish persecutors, that they had almost lost their religion. In India, both extremes of Moslem faith and practice may be found. The stately mosques of Delhi, Agra and Lahore conserve the orthodox worship, faith and practice as pure as they are in the mosques of Turkey and Syria. But in the villages and remote places, amid tribes who have never been well instructed, many practices will be found which are foreign to orthodox Islam.

In attempting, therefore, to give an account of Islam in India and the Far East, it seems best that I should begin by a brief statement in regard to Islam in general and show what is the rule of faith and practice among the two hundred and thirty million Mohammedans in the world. Such a presentation will also enable us better to appreciate the problem of their evangelisation. Besides, it is only fair that we should see the Moslem as he sees himself.

To the Moslem, Islam is the only true religion. It is God's revelation, made to Adam and all the antediluvian patriarchs and saints. It was the religion of Abraham and Moses, of David and the prophets of Israel, and of Jesus and the twelve apostles. When this true religion became corrupt and the world was given over to idolatry, it was once more revealed in its purity to Mohammed through the medium of the Quran. To the Moslem, therefore, Islam comprehends the faith of all dispensations. It is the religion of the genii and the angels, and shall only find its consummation in eternity.

Islam may be called the religion of submission to God. Every Moslem professes to have "placed his neck under the yoke of God." His boast is that he is a Mussulman, one who has submitted himself to God. This religion, like that of the Christian, is an exclusive religion. It admits none other as true. Indeed, it claims that Islam is true Christianity, that it is the Christianity of Christ. The modern Moslem controversialist endeavours to show that Paul was the real author of Gentile Christianity. From this standpoint, Christianity is a Moslem heresy, just as almost all mediæval Christian writers down to the Reformation declared Mohammedanism to be a Christian heresy. Moslem doctors tell us of four pillars of their faith: the Quran; the Traditions (*Ahadis*); the unanimous consent of the learned, (*Ijma*); and analogous reasoning based upon the Quran, the Traditions and the teaching of the learned (*Qiyas*).

The Quran is believed to be the word of God in the sense that every word, jot, and tittle is a matter of divine revelation. The original is inscribed upon the preserved table (*Luh-i-mahfuz*), which is kept under the throne of God. From this table the Quran was copied by the angel Gabriel and committed to Mohammed, who thus became the mouthpiece of God.

It may be of interest to repeat here the story of Mohammed's call to recite the Quran as told among Moslems in all lands. He had been living in a cave near the City of Mecca, where he spent the days and nights in devotion and prayer. One day he came home and told his wife Khadijah in great trepidation that he had a vision. He then said "Wrap me up! wrap me up!" She wrapped him up in a cloak and comforted him until his fear was dispelled. Then he said that the angel Gabriel had come to him in the cave and commanded him to read. He replied, "I am not a reader." "Then," said Mohammed, "the angel took hold of me and squeezed me as much as I could bear, and he let me go and said, 'Read.' And I said, 'I am not a reader.' Then he took hold of me and again squeezed me as much as I could bear and said:

> "Read! in the name of thy God who created man,
> Read! for thy Lord is most beneficent;
> He hath taught men the use of the pen;
> He hath taught man that which he knoweth not."

After hearing this story, and learning that her husband feared he was going to die, or that he was subject to some demoniacal possession, the faithful Khadijah said to him, "No, it will not be so. I swear by God he will never make you melancholy or sad. For verily you are kind to your relatives, you speak the truth, you are faithful in trusts, you bear the afflictions of the people, you spend in good works what you gain in trade, you are hospitable, and you assist your fellow-men." She then took him to her cousin Waraka, who was reputed a holy man,[1] and acquainted with the Jewish Scriptures. To him the story of the vision was repeated. Waraka then said, "This is the *Namus* which God sent to Moses." By this statement Waraka meant that Mohammed was now the subject of inspiration. And here began his prophetic career.

From this time forth during the space of a score of years, the revelations claimed by Mohammed were recorded and committed to memory by his followers and treasured up as the word of God. They were given out piecemeal and were usually adapted to the circumstances of the Prophet and his followers. The messages were often announced when some exigency of the new faith or of his personal interests required. At Mecca the revelations condemned the idols in the national pantheon, and vindicated the unity of the Godhead by reference to the testimony of nature and the consciences of men.

The preaching of Mohammed gave great offence to the tribe of the Koreish, which was recognised as the principal tribe of Mecca and had long been the custodian of the idol temple, the sacred Kaabah. They laughed at him and called him a madman. They could not do more, because he was under the protection of

[1] Waraka has been supposed to have been a Jew, but the probability is he was an Arab who, with Mohammed and others (Hanifs), had studied the Scriptures of the Jews and Christians to find the religion of Abraham.

powerful relatives. But they persecuted his followers and even threatened them with death. The Quran carefully notes these facts, and rebukes and threatens the persecutors with the vengeance of heaven. It tells them of the experiences of former prophets—how they were mocked and persecuted by the unbelievers, how God in his mercy warned them, how he wrought miracles before them, and how the blinded wretches rejected the signs and rushed on to destruction. Some were swallowed up by an earthquake. Others were drowned in a flood. Once a hot wind blew upon a slumbering city, leaving its inhabitants corpses. Again a plague destroyed the enemies of God and his prophets. The Jews were reminded of the fate of unbelievers among them in the olden time.

Up to this point Mohammed stood as a witness for God and bore the oppositions of his countrymen with much patience and forbearance. But at Medina the circumstances of the Prophet were entirely changed. Jews and Arabs greeted him with gladness. There was none now to persecute him or his followers. Even the refugees to the court of the Abyssinian King now returned and gathered around their Prophet. Here the revelations began to speak in a conciliatory tone. The Jews were even flattered. The Moslems were commanded to pray toward Jerusalem. The Old Testament Scriptures were commended in terms of great praise. But all this was lost on the Jews. They would not recognise the prophetical claims of this Arab apostle. They soon began to ridicule his pretensions and finally denounced him as an impostor.

The tone of the Quran now changed in its messages concerning the Jews. They were now declared to be a people accursed of God, because they had persecuted and even killed the prophets of God. The temple at Jerusalem was now abandoned and the Kaabah of Mecca was chosen as the Kibla toward which the faithful should pray. Christians were now spoken of kindly. Their charity was praised. Jesus was declared to be a prophet of God. His purity of character and wonderful miracles were extolled.

By this time the new faith had gained many adherents from among the Arabs, Jews, and Christians. But a new adversary arose in the person of Abdullah-Ibn-Ubbai, the chief of a powerful faction in Medina, who was jealous of the growing influence of Mohammed, He and his party now received the special attention of Mohammed's genius of inspiration. The need of the Prophet for divine guidance seemed to greatly increase. The voice of Gabriel was continually ringing in his ears. Sometimes (he said) the voice was like the sound of a bell, sometimes like the roar of a tornado; at other times an angel appeared before him in the form of one of his attendants and spoke to him in an audible voice. Now came a command to attack a Meccan caravan. Then an order came relating to the Moslems; perhaps to regulate their social intercourse, their treatment of their wives, their neighbours, or their Prophet. At another time prayer and fasting were instituted, or some old Arab custom was abolished. More than once Gabriel came to the Prophet's relief with his copies of the heavenly records. Once this occurred when Mohammed fell in love with the beautiful wife of Zaid, his adopted son. When Zaid heard of it he put away his wife, so that his benefactor might marry her. But Arab custom declared the thing scandalous. Now came a revelation from heaven by which Mohammed was commanded to marry the divorced Zainab, "in order that henceforth the faithful may not be bound by the old custom forbidding men to marry the divorced wives of their adopted sons."[2] On another occasion the ancient custom of the Arabs that no one should carry on a warfare during sacred months was violated by a marauding band of the Moslems. The thing caused great excitement, even among Mohammed's followers. The offending Moslems were arrested and the booty placed in bond until the will of God could be learned. Soon after Gabriel appeared to the Prophet declaring that infidelity was worse than warring in sacred months, and that henceforth unbelievers would have no immunity from attack in the sacred months. Accordingly the prisoners were released and rewarded, and the booty divided between the Prophet and his marauding followers. On still another occasion Gabriel was invoked to shield the favourite wife Ayesha from the tongue of scandal.

Such is the character of the revelations of the Quran. So intimate is the relation between the matter of revelation and the life and experience of the Prophet that a knowledge of the latter is necessary to any intelligent understanding of the former.

At the death of Mohammed the various portions of the Quran were found in a box which had been committed to the care of one of his wives. They were

[2] *Quran*, Chap. xxxiii. 37.

written upon palm leaves and white stones. Some of the Moslems, too, possessed copies, and some had committed the whole to memory. Lest these records should be lost, the Caliph Abu Bekr appointed Zaid-Ibn-Sabit, one of Mohammed's amanuenses, to compile the Quran. This copy afterward underwent slight revision to make the idiom everywhere correspond with that of the Koreishite tribe of Mecca. The book thus compiled contains 114 *Suras* or chapters. These are not recorded in their chronological order, but, somewhat after the manner of the prophetical books of the Jewish Scriptures, the longer chapters were placed first and the shorter last—the whole being introduced by a prayer.

There is much uncertainty in regard to the compilation of the Quran. A careful examination of the chapters based upon the best authorities shows their complex character; portions of a chapter having been revealed in Mecca and other portions belonging to Medina. Take, for instance, the second chapter (The Cow). The sections of this chapter belong as follows: vs. 1-20 belong to Medina; vs. 21-38 to Mecca; vs. 39-163 to Medina; vs. 164-172 to Mecca; vs. 173-253 to Medina; vs. 254-257 probably to Mecca; vs. 258-284 to Medina, and finally, vs. 285-286 to Mecca. Even these subdivisions are made up of smaller sections revealed at the same place in different years.

If that passage in Daniel, viii. 23, in regard to "A king of fierce countenance and understanding dark sentences," be rightly interpreted as referring to Mohammed, we may truly describe the Quran as a book of "dark sentences." A few passages, like the oases in the deserts of Arabia, stand out as truly beautiful both in their setting and in their thought. Take the first chapter, the *Fatihat:*

> "In the name of God, the compassionate, the merciful.
> Praise be to God, Lord of all the worlds!
> The compassionate, the merciful!
> King on the Day of Judgment!
> Thee do we worship, and to thee do we cry for help!
> Guide then us in the right way!
> The path of those to whom thou art gracious!
> Not of those with whom thou art angered, nor of those who go astray."

The celebrated throne verse in Chap. II., 255, is as follows: "God! there is no God but he; the living, the self-subsisting: neither slumber nor sleep seizeth him; to him belongeth whatsoever is in heaven and on earth. Who is he that can intercede with him, but through his good pleasure? He knoweth that which is past, and that which is to come unto them, and they shall not comprehend anything of his knowledge, but so far as he pleaseth. His throne is extended over heaven and earth, and the preservation of both is no burden unto him. He is high, the Mighty."

The question is often asked why a book of such singular composition should hold such sway over the millions of the Moslem world. In reply two reasons may be given: first, the beautiful rhythm, and often sweet cadences of the original language, which like some enchanting song hold multitudes with rapt attention who understand scarcely a word they hear;

secondly, there is a vast amount of truth contained in the book, especially the truth of the divine unity and of man's dependence upon God, as seen in the throne verse just now quoted.

The second great pillar of Islam is the *Hadith* or Traditions. These are sometimes called the *Sunnat,* or manner of life. They sum up the sayings, doings, and permissions of Mohammed in regard to various matters, were collected and recorded in their present form two or three centuries after his death, and are arranged under four principal heads:

1. The things said by Mohammed.

2. Things done by Mohammed in the presence of his followers.

3. Things done by disciples in the presence of the Prophet and against which he did not show any disapprobation.

4. Things done in Mohammed's presence which he condemned. This mass of matter has been compiled in six great volumes called the Six Correct Books, (as *Sihah-As-Sittah*).

The compilation of Moslem traditions afforded a wide sphere for the imagination of the relators, not to say the exploitation of pure fiction wherever personal notoriety or interest was concerned. With all the care of the collectors and the warning of Mohammed himself, Moslem scholars admit that many spurious traditions have been handed down. Abu Daud, one of the collectors, rejected all but forty-eight hundred traditions out of five hundred thousand which were submitted to him. Out of forty thousand persons who have been instrumental in handing down traditions, Al-Bukhari only acknowledged two thousand as authoritative. On this account these traditions are classified in three great divisions, genuine, mediocre and weak. It will be seen that we have here a most fruitful source of debate as to the relative value of any tradition. The principles established to distinguish between genuine and spurious traditions were somewhat peculiar. The chain of witnesses for each and every tradition must be composed of links, each one of which was a pious Moslem of sound mind, discreet, sober, and clear-headed. If all the witnesses were able to stand this test, the tradition was accepted and marked genuine. If there were doubts about one or more of the witnesses, the tradition, though accepted, was marked "weak" or "doubtful."

The following will give an idea of the form and character of these traditions:

"Abu Kuraib said to us that Ibrahim-Ibn-Yusuf-Ibn-Abu-Ishak said to us, from his father, from Abu-Ishak, from Tulata-Ibn Musarif that he said, I have heard, from Abdur-Rahman-Ibn-Ausajah, that he said, I have heard that the Prophet said, *Whosoever shall give in charity a milch cow, or silver, or a leathern bottle of water, it shall be equal to the freeing of a slave.*"

Here we have a complete chain of witnesses between the Prophet and the narrator of the tradition. The degree of inspiration accorded to the Traditions is not unlike that which we accord to the New Testament Scriptures. The Prophet is conceived as speaking under the influence of a divine guidance operating upon his mind and heart.

As the Quran is the main source of authority in doctrine, so the Traditions are the chief source of knowledge in respect to all questions of practice. The ceremonies and customs relating to prayer, fasting, almsgiving, pilgrimage, marriage, burial of the dead, and even matters of dress and adornment, the cut of the beard, the dye of the hair, and the wood of a tooth brush—all are controlled by the dictum of the Traditions as interpreted by the learned. Suppose, for instance, a dog should be drowned in a well, the question of purification would have to be settled by reference to the men steeped in traditional lore. These doctors would consult the great tomes of Traditions and the commentators thereon, and by and by they would say just how many gallons of water would have to be drawn out from the well before it could be regarded as pure.

The third pillar of Moslem faith, called *Ijma,* the consensus of the learned, is a collection of the opinions of the *mujtahids* or learned among the companions of the Prophet and the *ansars,* or helpers, who were converted at Medina during Mohammed's ministry there, and the disciples and companions of both of these classes. Naturally it was believed that such men were in a position best to understand what was meant by the words of the Quran, and especially by the sayings of their Prophet preserved in the Traditions. It was stipulated as a cardinal principle that these opinions of the learned should on no account contradict the teaching of the Quran or the Traditions; but, when they do agree with these, they are regarded as authoritative in all questions of interpretation and law.

The fourth pillar of the Moslem faith is called *Qiyas*. By this term is meant the analogical reasoning of the learned as to the teaching of the Quran, the Traditions, and the *Ijma*. Here we find a place for the exercise of the reason in matters of faith and practice. Four great schools of interpretation have grown up, whose teachings have practically created so many sects among the Moslems. These school and their founders are as follows:

1. The Hanafiyahs, a sect founded by Imam Abu Hanifa, a great oracle of Moslem jurisprudence, born at Busra, A. D. 702. Abu Hanifa spent most of his life in Kufa, the capital of Irak. He based his teachings upon the *ipsissima verba* of the Quran, "For to thee have we sent down the book which cleareth up everything" (Chap. xvi. 91). "Nothing have we passed over in the book" (Chap. vi. 38). "Neither is there a grain in the darkness of the earth, nor a green or sere, but it is noted in a distinct writing" (Chap. vi. 59). These texts were held to prove that all law was provided for by anticipation in the Quran. Of Abu Hanifa's system a writer in the *Journal Asiatique* (4me serie, tome xi) says, "The merit of logical fearlessness cannot be denied to it. The wants and wishes of men, the previous history of a country—all those considerations, in fact, which are held in the West to be the governing principles of legislation, are set aside by the legists of Irak as being of no account whatever. Legislation is not a science inductive and experimental, but logical and deductive." [3]

2. The Malikiyahs, a sect founded by Imam Ibn

[3] Sell's *Faith of Islam*, p. 20.

Malik, who was born at Medina, A. D. 714. His system was largely based upon the Traditions, and was, therefore, historical in its character, exalting the Traditions to a level with the Quran.

3. The Shafiayahs, a sect founded by Imam As Shafii, who was born in Askelon in Palestine, A. D. 767. He passed his youth in Mecca, but finally settled in Cairo in Egypt, where he died. His system was eclectic, and forms a compromise between his predecessors, basing his teachings upon both the Quran and the six great volumes of Moslem Traditions.

4. The Hanbaliyahs were a sect founded by Imam Ibn Hanbal, who was born at Bagdad, A. D. 780. His system was a reaction against the rationalising teaching based upon the analogical deductions of the system of Abu Hanifa. Ibn Hanbal abolished the principle of analogical deduction altogether, and so discarded reason from all theological or legal discussion. The exact declaration of the Quran on the Traditions could be the only source of knowledge. This sect has no existence in India except as it is represented by the Wahabis.

These four sects have many subdivisions which need not be mentioned unless it be that of the Mutazilites, which have had a recent recrudescence among the more progressive Mohammedans of this generation.

The great mass of Moslem doctors, however, no longer undertake to learn for themselves just what the Quran and the Traditions really teach, but strive to discover what the learned fathers say they teach.

Reason has been virtually ruled out of court and

dogmatism in its worst sense has obtained supremacy over Moslem minds.

Let us now turn to the creed. This, according to Moslem authorities, includes seven points enumerated in the following formula:

"I believe in God, in the Angels, in the Books, in the Apostles, in the Last Day, in the Decrees of Almighty God, both as respects good and evil, and in the Resurrection after death."

Faith in God is not only belief in his being as a personal God, but especially in his absolute unity. It excludes not only plurality of deities, but also plurality of persons in the One God. It repudiates every thought of incarnation, and is therefore totally opposed to the Christian doctrine of the Trinity and of the Incarnation of God in Jesus Christ. Of the Divine attributes, Islam recognises "Life, Wisdom, Power, Will, Hearing, Seeing, and Speaking." The Moslem thought of God is thus described by Stanley Lane Poole: "He is the Lord of the world, the author of the heavens and the earth, who hath created life and death, in whose hands is dominion, who maketh the dawn to appear and causeth the night to cover the day, the great all-powerful Lord of the Glorious Throne; the thunder proclaimeth his perfection, the whole earth is his handful, and the heavens shall be folded together in his right hand. And with this power he conceives the knowledge that directs it to right ends. God is the wise, the just, the true, the swift in reckoning, who knoweth every ant's weight of good and of ill that each man hath done, and who suffereth not the reward of the faithful to perish."

So overwhelming is the sense of the power of the Almighty that there seems to be no room left for the will of the creature, and so it comes to pass that in the minds of the majority of Moslems "God plays with humanity as on a chess-board, and works out his game without regard to the sacrifice of the pieces."

And yet we must not rush to the conclusion that Islam has no place for the mercy of God. However, mercy is not the chief thought of Islam, although almost every chapter of the Quran begins "in the name of God, merciful and beneficent." And yet it remains true that the Moslem is guided by fear, rather than drawn by love.

The God of Islam is undoubtedly the true God, but as Christians we object to the Moslem's conception of him. We object to his having exalted God's omnipotence over all other attributes. We object to the lowering of God's character for holiness, nothing being said of this in the Quran which might not be said of a holy man. We object to the habit of limiting the goodness of God to Moslems, no matter what their character and conduct may be. And finally, we object to the sacrifice of God's justice by denying the necessity for any atonement for sin.

There is one fact in regard to the Moslem's thought of God, which has led some Christian writers to deny that the Allah of Islam is the true God; this is that the Allah of the Quran is not only the God who is lauded in the Quran, as we have already shown, but the God who speaks in every word, syllable and letter of the Quran. According to Islam, Mohammed was but the mouthpiece of Divinity. If, then, we would get a correct idea of the Moslem's concept of God, we must take into account all that was done by Mohammed under the sanction of the Quran. Let this be done and it will appear that what we have just said about the Mohammedan concept of God is by no means extravagant.

In regard to the word of God, the Moslem believes in one hundred and four volumes of sacred Scripture revealed through the medium of prophets, closing with the Quran given to Mohammed. Of these, one hundred are no longer extant on earth. Of these again ten were given to Adam, fifty to Seth, thirty to Enoch, and ten to Abraham. The four Books extant are the Pentateuch of Moses, the Psalms of David, the Gospel of Jesus, and the Quran of Mohammed. These four Books are all recognised by the Quran as the word of God, given for a light to guide men into the way of salvation. Moslems, however, unable to reconcile the Quran with the former books, deny their genuineness. When, therefore, a Moslem says he believes in the books of the Christian Scriptures, he means only to declare that such books were once delivered to the prophets, but are now so corrupted as no longer to be worthy of credence excepting in so far as they are confirmed by the Quran.

As to the apostles and prophets, through whom the scriptures have been given, Moslems believe in one hundred and forty-four thousand. Of these, however, we find mention in the Quran of only twenty-eight. Nine of these are designated as leaders in the ushering in of new dispensations. Of these nine, six are called great prophets (*Nabi-ul-Azim*). They are Adam, Noah, Abraham, Moses, Jesus and Mohammed. A striking fact in regard to these prophets is that although the orthodox belief is that all were sinless, yet the testimony of both the Quran and the Traditions is that Jesus was the only sinless prophet. Of all others, the testimony of Moslem scripture is that they either confessed their sins or that God commanded them to do so. This is most especially true of Mohammed, who is commanded to confess and repent of his sins. "Know, therefore, that there is no god but God; and ask pardon for thy sins, and for the true believers both men and women" (Chap. xlviii. 21). "Ask pardon of God, since God is indulgent and merciful" (Chap. iv. 105). "Ask pardon for thy fault, and celebrate the praise of thy Lord in the evening and in the morning" (Chap. xi. 57). "Verily we have granted thee a manifest victory, that God may forgive thee thy preceding and thy subsequent sins," etc. (Chap xlviii. 1-3).

In the Traditions we have the following among many passages, representing Mohammed as seeking for the pardon of his sins: "Verily, I ask pardon of God, and turn from sin toward him, more than seventy times daily," "I ask pardon of God one hundred times a day." (*Mishqat ul Musabih,* Book X, Chap. iii, part 1). But of Jesus, nowhere is there a line or even a suggestion of any sort that He was ever chargeable with sin. JESUS IS THE ONLY SINLESS PROPHET OF ISLAM. This fact is of inestimable value to the cause of Moslem evangelisation. Given a sinless Jesus, now exalted in heaven, and destined to come again to rescue the faithful from the powers of Dajjal, the Moslem Antichrist, and the question of his claim to be the Saviour of sinners is practically decided in his favour.

Of all the great doctrines of Islam no one impresses itself more powerfully upon the Moslem mind than the doctrine of the Resurrection and the Judgment Day. To Moslems this is the great day of assizes. The day will be at least one thousand years in duration. Its approach will be marked by many signs; the faith will decay among men, wickedness and corruption will be rampant, the meanest persons shall be advanced to exalted dignity, there will be tumults and seditions, wars and distress in the world; the sun shall rise in the West and a horrible beast shall arise out of the earth and appear in the holy temple of Mecca. Antichrist, the One-Eyed One, with the word *Kafir* (Infidel), written on his forehead, will then appear in Syria, riding on a white ass, followed by seventy thousand Jews. He shall continue on the earth for fourteen months, conquering and devastating until he be destroyed by Jesus, who shall descend from heaven and establish the true religion throughout the whole world. These with many other marvellous signs shall portend the near approach of the awful day when the first blast of the angel trumps shall strike terror to every heart in heaven and earth. A second blast will visit with death every creature in the universe. The third trumpet blast of the angel, now himself raised from the dead, will restore all to life. Then the judgment will begin.

Then shall every beast that has suffered at the hands of a cruel master tread upon the prostrate form of his persecutor. Then shall the wicked be brought forth with blackened faces, backbiters in the form of apes, tyrants in the form of swine, hypocrites gnawing their tongues, the proud and vainglorious clad in garments daubed with pitch. These shall be obliged to pass over a bridge so narrow that they shall step off it into the gaping vortex of hell underneath.

The righteous, by which we are to understand the faithful of every age and dispensation, shall be brought forth in honour, clad in bright and beautiful garments, seated on white camels with saddles of gold. To them shall be opened the gates of Paradise, into which they shall be ushered. There they shall be seated on sofas garnished with silk and precious stones, and shall disport themselves in the companionship of the black-eyed girls of Paradise eating the luscious fruits of Eden, and drinking the spicy waters of *Al Kauthar* out of vessels of gold.

This is the vision which lures the Moslem warrior to martyrdom. This is his crown of rejoicing.

We must now turn to the practical duties imposed upon Moslems by the tenets of their faith. They are summed up under five heads: the reciting of the *Kalima,* observing of the stated prayers, fasting, giving of alms and pilgrimage to Mecca. By reciting the *Kalima* is meant repeating the formula *La ilāha illā'-'llāhu: Muhammadur Rasūlu'llah.* "There is no deity but God: Mohammed is the apostle of God." This formula must be repeated at least once before death, with a sincere heart and a loud voice in the presence of witnesses.

The duty of prayer requires the regular observance of the five daily stated prayers. At the first streak of dawn, the muezzin announces the time of the first daily prayer. The next prayer must be offered about midday. The third call to prayer occurs about three o'clock in the afternoon. The time for the fourth prayer is fixed at about sunset. The fifth prayer should be offered when the night has closed in. These prayers should be uttered in the Arabic language, and if possible the men should assemble in a mosque for that purpose. They may be, and, indeed, generally are, offered wherever the Moslem may be at the prayer hour. It is an impressive scene to witness them as they drop their implements of daily toil and either in companies or alone spread a sheet upon the ground and proceed to say their prayers. It may be on the roadside or at a railway station, no matter where, no matter by whom surrounded, the Moslem says his prayers. His witness for his faith is clear. He glories in his faith.

On Friday, they are expected to attend the mosque for public worship. Here special prayers suited to their holy day are offered. Sometimes the service is accompanied by a discourse or sermon. When the Friday papers are concluded, the Moslem returns to his usual occupation.

The duty of fasting relates particularly to the fast of Ramazan. This is a sacred month. During this month every Moslem should fast from sunrise until sunset. No morsel of food or drop of water may pass his lips during the day. This in hot climates in the long days of summer is a serious trial. Many lose their health and some their lives through the rigour of this fast. Sick and weakly persons are exempt on condition they fast an equal number of days at another time. During the night the Moslem is free to eat and drink as much as he pleases.

Almsgiving is based upon a kind of legal taxation, something like the tithe system of the Jews. It is assessed variously according to the employment of the giver. It amounts to two and a half per cent. of his gains or income, and is spent in the cause of religion and the support of the poor. It must not be inferred from this law that this is the sum total of Moslem charity. They are generous and kind to the poor, and hospitable to travellers and strangers.

Pilgrimage to Mecca, like the duty of prayer, fasting, and almsgiving, is enjoined by the teaching of the Quran and sanctioned by the example of the Prophet. Every Moslem with health and money sufficient to enable him to perform the pilgrimage must do so at least once in his lifetime. Where the people are poor they combine together and raise a fund sufficient to send one of their number as a representative pilgrim.

The rites connected with pilgrimage to Mecca are a relic of Arab heathenism, but are purged of all idolatrous sentiment. The rite which most nearly approaches to the idolatrous is that of kissing the Black Stone in the corner of the Kaabah or sacred temple.

Absurd as many of the rites of pilgrimage seem to be, there is nothing in Islam that does so much to conserve the spirit and the unity of Islam among the nations.[4] The thousands and tens of thousands who take part in the rites of the holy pilgrimage at Mecca, return to their homes as holy men among their fellows. Henceforth they are designated as Hajjis and are looked upon by the common people as authoritative sources of information on all religious questions. Often they are filled with a new and fiery zeal for the reformation of abuses and the propagation of the faith among the idolatrous. To these five stated duties of Islam, we should also add that of *Jihad,* Crusade or Religious War. The use of the word *Jihad,* in those chapters of the Quran which were written at Mecca before the Hejira, suggested nothing more than effort or endeavour. It had then no suggestion of warring and bloodshed. It had relation to whatever could be used or done by the faithful for the promotion or defence of Islam.

When, however, Mohammed found himself in Medina clothed with secular power, and could send

[4] "One of the benefits of their pilgrimage, and perhaps the greatest of all if we regard the sacrament either from the political or social or from the religious standpoint, was, and is, the gathering together in Mecca of Mohammedans of every race and of every sect. There, and in the City of Medina, they first saw the dawn of their religious faith and their political power; there their hearts were drawn together in unity and strength; and there in the early days of the Caliph, they discussed their latest achievements, the glory of their future conquests, and studied the wants and needs of their co-religionists.—Thus Mecca, in the days of pilgrimage, might be looked upon as an immense club or a university, where Mohammedans, from every quarter of the globe, meet and discuss their political and social problems." (Hadji Khan, M. R. A. S., in his book *With the Pilgrims to Mecca,* p. 29.)

forth his followers armed to fight against his enemies, the word *Jihad* suggested war against the enemies of Islam. And when, by and by, he determined to conquer his native city and set up Islam as the national religion, the same term was used to express the idea of war against unbelievers for the advancement of the Moslem faith. Four months had been given to the idolaters of Mecca to adjust themselves to the new regime. After that the command given to the Moslems was to be carried out. It ran as follows: "And when the sacred months are passed, kill those who join other gods with God wherever ye find them; and seize them, besiege them, and lay wait for them with every kind of ambush; but if they shall convert, and observe prayer, and pay the obligatory alms, then let them go their way, for God is gracious and merciful" (Quran, Chap. ix. 5-6). And again the command concerning Jews and Christians: "Make war upon such of those to whom the Scriptures have been given as believe not in God, or in the last day, and forbid not that which God and his apostle have forbidden, and who profess the profession of the truth, until they pay tribute (*Jizyah*) out of hand, and they be humbled" (Quran, Chap. ix. 29).

These passages, with others of like import, impose upon Moslems a duty, which accounts for those wars of conquest which have filled the earth with blood, and which have accounted for much of the success which has accompanied the mission of the Arabian prophet. This command requires that every Moslem hold himself ready to fight in the way of God. This either means to fight in defence of the faith or, under competent guidance, to make war upon the infidels with a view to their conversion or extirpation. When war has been entered upon and a people or tribe is overcome, the option is given to the survivors either of accepting Islam or of paying tribute. Refusal to do either was to be punished by death. Out of this attitude of Islam to the outside world have grown many dreadful consequences. First among these is the death penalty for apostasy from Islam. Then the failure of those who submit to pay *Jizyah* or poll tax [6] to fulfil the condition, or the perpetration of any act which could be interpreted as a refusal to obey the rulers, would be the signal for assault upon the entire community as enemies of the state and infidels before God. An illustration of this was the slaughter of Armenians in Turkey in 1895 and the whole catalogue of horrible atrocities which have since occurred. It is under shelter of this doctrine of *Jihad* that Mohammedans have always felt justified in assaulting any nation or tribe of unbelievers. It was under shelter of this principle that Arab slave-hunters did their bloody work in Central Africa.

The reflex influence of *Jihad* or religious war upon the Moslem peoples of the world has been to make them indifferent to bloodshed. The atrocities which have filled the Christian world with horror, have failed to arouse among them anywhere the least feeling of resentment.

Such then, is the religion of Islam, concerning whose votaries in India and the Far East we shall discourse in the following chapters. Like every other religion

[6] Amounting to $2.50 annually for each adult male.

it has been influenced by the national life and customs of the nations and races among whom it has been propagated. India and China and the islands of Malaysia afford many illustrations of this fact. Like Christianity, Islam has been divided by schisms and heresies. Some of these sects have been based upon political, others upon doctrinal grounds. They number about one hundred and fifty. Of the sects, which have been stamped as heterodox on theological grounds, the Ali-Illahis have done much to prepare the way for the incoming of the Gospel. They believe that God was incarnate in the various Imams or Leaders in all dispensations down to the time of Ali, who was the last. Here we notice how the thought of incarnation has imposed itself upon the bald unitarianism of Islam.

Still another sect, the Mushabiites, taught that God possessed a human form.

The Mutazillites rejected the doctrine of the eternity of the Quran and insisted upon the place of reason in discussing its doctrines.

The sect of the Sufis, or Mystics, adopt a pantheistic philosophy and endeavour to explain the Quran in accord with it. The result is a seemingly spiritual worship on the one hand, and a blind fatalism, amounting to atheism, on the other. The influence of these various heterodox schools of thought upon the Moslem mind is of no small moment to the cause of Christian evangelisation. These elements of Mohammedan nationality afford some very hopeful subjects of missionary endeavour.

On its theological side, Islam is supported by an

extensive literature in the Arabic language, most of which has been translated into Persian, Hindustani, and other Indian languages. At specified centres it has schools for the training of its mullahs and maulvies. One such school, the Al-Azhar, in Cairo, Egypt, with 12,000 students from all parts of the Moslem world, exercises much influence in India and the Far East. In India, China, Sumatra, and Java many schools have been established under the patronage of princes and kings, nobles and wealthy men, where Moslem youth are being educated. Thus the religion of Islam, holding sway over at least two hundred and thirty millions of Moslems constituting one-seventh of the population of the globe, second only to Christianity in numerical strength among the religions of the world and occupying many of the chief centres of influence in the Eastern world, commands respect, in spite of its appalling errors. It is indeed the only rival of Christianity for universal supremacy.

This condition should serve to startle the Christian world. Missionary societies should give it most careful thought, men specially suited by education and temperament should be sent into the mission fields located in Moslem countries, with a view to their making a special study of the languages and literature, so as to be able strongly to influence the Moslem mind in their preaching and teaching. As the Spirit chose men specially fitted by education and training for the work of evangelising the Greek and Roman Empire, let us pray God to send forth many men especially suited to the work of Moslem evangelisation.

II

THE MOSLEM CONQUEST OF INDIA

To fully understand the problem of Moslem evangelisation in India and the Far East, it is necessary to inquire as to the history of the advent of Islam into these regions and so arrive at an understanding of the conditions which beset the endeavour to evangelise these followers of Mohammed. To arrive at this knowledge, we propose to take a brief survey of the Moslem conquest of India.

The religious condition of India's millions in the eighth century of the Christian Era was that of a people wholly given to idolatry. Everywhere the Brahmanical hierarchy held supreme control. The ruling chiefs everywhere accorded them reverence. No event in the affairs of state could be undertaken without the consent and the blessing of the priesthood. Caste ruled the people with an iron hand, and yet it was caste that divided them into many sections or factions, each in general quite indifferent to the other. Any great danger, threatening the common weal, would avail to unite the ruling chiefs and at once bring into the field an army of the most formidable proportions. It was, however, always an army composed of units so loosely bound together as to admit of rapid disintegration. Every tribe was under the domination of a despot. The priesthood tyrannised over all. The vast hordes of the aboriginal and outcaste tribes were treated with a contempt worse than that of slavery. The great mass of the people lived in the most abject poverty, whilst the idols of gold and silver were adorned with diamonds and rubies. The temples were often covered with sheets of gold, while the priests and rulers dwelt in luxury. India possessed a people and a rule, combining the elements of both weakness and strength. She was strong in the fearless courage of her Rajput soldiery, but weak in her social fabric, which might at any time fall to pieces and avail to strengthen the enemy rather than to defeat the foe.

This brief statement will illustrate, and to some degree make plain how it came about that a mere handful of marauders were able to establish themselves in the borders of India and by and by to impose upon her people a foreign rule and to domicile a foreign religion.

When the armies of Moslems began to pour forth from Arabia for the conquest of the world, India and the lands farther east were hardly within the thought of these zealots. The rich treasure and possible plunder of the Greek and Persian empires were enough to engross their attention for a generation at least, and but for the fanatical zeal of Al-Hajaj, the governor of Chaldea, it is doubtful whether the Arabian Empire under the Caliphs would have had any part in the propagation of Islam in India.

Al-Hajaj sent an expedition to India in the year 711 A. D., under the leadership of his cousin Mohammed Qasim, a youth of but seventeen years, accompanied by twelve thousand warriors mounted on horses and camels. Marching along the coast of Persia this army made its way to the City of Daibul, "the great mediaeval port of the Indus valley, the forerunner of Karachi."[1] Many accessions were made to this force from the warlike tribes interviewed by the way. Boats bearing catapults and other materials of war were sent by sea, and soon the city was besieged. A red flag floated from the top of a tall temple. This was made the special object of attack and soon the flagstaff was shattered by a shot from the great catapult named "The Bride." "The fall of the sacred flag dismayed the garrison; a sortie was repulsed with loss; the Moslems brought ladders and scaled the walls, and the place was carried by assault. The governor fled, the Brahmans were butchered, and after three days of carnage a Mohammedan quarter was laid out, a mosque built, and a garrison of four thousand men detached to hold the city."[2] The victorious army pushed its way up the right bank of the Indus and soon, discovering the army of the Hindus, put themselves in battle array. A fierce battle ensued, which ended in the flight of the Hindus, whose king was slain. Another battle at Brahmanabad, and Multan, the chief city of the Indus Valley, surrendered after a long siege. "The fighting men were massacred; the priests, workmen, women, and children made captives."[3] The Indus Valley lay at the feet of the Moslems.

This campaign is of special interest to us in this discussion because it is typical of every one of scores of similar expeditions made for the conquest of India by

[1] Stanley Lane Poole in *Mediaeval India*, p. 8.
[2] *Idem.* [3] *Idem.*

the warrior messengers of Islam. We see here the two-fold agency of the proselyting sword and the consequent conversion of the people to the new religion. The vast majority of the Arab soldiery were intent upon the booty, which the law of the Quran and the example of the Prophet awarded to the Moslem warrior. The law of the Quran provides that four-fifths of the spoils of war be divided among the soldiers who may have taken part in the battle; the remaining fifth to be given to the Prophet or his successors for the uses of the cause of Islam (Quran viii. 42).[4] The Caliph's purpose in sending forth such expeditions was to bring the nations under the dominion of the true religion. The command of Mohammed is given in the following words:

"When ye encounter the unbelievers, strike off their heads, until ye have made a great slaughter among them; and bind them in bonds; and either give them a free dismission afterwards, or exact a ransom; until the war shall have laid down its arms. This shall ye do." (Quran xlviii. 4, 5.) This passage is understood to mean that all persons fighting against Moslems are to be put to death, unless they accept Islam as their religion. If caught afterwards they may be ransomed or set at liberty or sold into captivity, as the captor pleaseth.

These provisions in the law of conquest account for the awful carnage which usually followed in the wake

[4] The *Hidayah* (vol. 88, p. 159), holds that the Prophet's fifth must be divided into three equal portions for the relief of orphans, the feeding of the poor, and the entertainment of travellers. Hughes' *Dictionary of Islam*, p. 459.

of Moslem victory. Three days of carnage followed the capture of Daibul. At Dahir, our historian tells us, "the Moslems were glutted with slaughter." So cruel were the conquerors, that the Hindu king's sister called the women together and "refusing to owe their lives to the vile 'cow eaters,' at the price of dishonour, they set their house ablaze and perished in the flames."[5] This contempt for the lives of the rebellious or vanquished was exemplified over and over in the history of Islam in India. The slave Emperor Balban once slew forty thousand Mongols, whom he suspected of disloyalty, notwithstanding they had professed the Moslem religion. Timur (Tamerlane) felt encumbered by one hundred thousand Hindu prisoners taken at the capture of Delhi. He ordered them to be slain in cold blood. The Bahmanid Mohammed I, son of Hassan Gangu, once avenged the death of his Moslem garrison at Mudkal, by the slaughter of seventy thousand helpless men, women and children. Such were the deeds of the proselyting sword, which was unsheathed against the unbelieving world by the mandate of the Prophet already quoted. Mohammed himself set the example in his campaigns against the Bani Nadhir, the Bani Qainuqaa and the Jews at Khaibar.

The effect of the Moslem conquest of Sindh, interpreted in the light of the law of Islam, may be indicated thus:

1. The unbelievers found fighting against the Moslems were either slain or doomed to death. The only hope of escape was acceptance of Islam, with the privilege of participating in future wars and the rewards of victory.

[5] *Mediaeval India*, p. 9.

2. The inhabitants, who remained, had the option of either embracing the new religion or of retaining their houses and lands upon payment of a capitation tax of about $2.50 per annum for every male person; women and children were excepted. Such persons were called *Zimmies.* They were exempt from military duty and dwelt under the protection of the Moslem government. They were permitted to practise religious rites and worship under certain limitations.[6]

3. As *Zimmies,* the subject population forfeited all the political and social privileges enjoyed by the ruling classes. Many of them were in government employ and often held responsible positions, but their tenure of office might cease at any moment. All this and much more renders the subject condition of an intelligent people well nigh intolerable. We see this illustrated by the case of the Armenian population of Turkey.

We have cited this law at this point because we shall see how it operated to promote the work of the mullahs as well as of the rulers, in their effort to convert the people of India to Islam. This, too, will suffice to illustrate the same process in other lands.

It must not be forgotten that many a Moslem ruler, like Mohammed Qasim the conqueror of Sindh, was anxious to establish good government over his subjects

[6] This law is based upon the following passage from the *Quran:* "Make war upon such of those to whom the scriptures have been given, as believe not in God or in the last day, and forbid not that which God and his apostles have forbidden, and who profess not the profession of truth, until they pay tribute (*Jizyah*) out of their hand, and they be humbled." (*Quran,* chap. ix. 29.)

within the boundaries of social and political requirement prescribed by the Law of Islam. In Sindh, "the citizens and villagers were allowed to furnish the tax collectors themselves; the Brahmans were protected and entrusted with high offices, for which their education made them indispensable; and the conqueror's instructions to all his officers were wise and conciliatory: 'Deal honestly,' he commanded, 'between the people and the governor; if there be distribution, distribute equitably, and fix the revenues according to the ability to pay. Be in concord among yourselves, and wrangle not, that the country be not vexed.'"[7] Nor must it be forgotten that the great purpose of these great wars against the infidels was, at least in these early years of Moslem aggression, to establish the religion of Islam upon the ruins of idolatry. The story of the most bloody battles and the indiscriminate slaughter of the people in the conquered cities is always followed by an account of the building of mosques, the establishment of schools for the teaching of the Quran and the religious training of the new converts and their children. Any study of Mohammedanism which overlooks the intense zeal of the Moslem in the propagation of his faith, is sadly defective. The Christian evangelist, who would carry the Gospel into Moslem lands, will soon discover that his chief obstacle is not the temporal power of the hierarchy, but the intense hold which Islam has upon its votaries. Call it bigotry, if you will, and bigotry there is without doubt, but that something which stands behind this fanaticism is the power which deserves his special attention. That *something* is un-

[7] *Mediaeval India*, p. 10.

doubtedly the fundamental strength of Islam—the knowledge of God as a personal God, having all power, who claims allegiance and unquestioning submission to himself as the only object of worship. The Moslem believes himself to be the object of his special favour, and at the time when the armed hosts of Islam went forth to fight the enemies of the true God, their constant success in crushing the idolaters was to them the witness of God to the truth of their religion. And when to this we add the consideration that Islam in India was confronted by one of the grossest forms of idolatry the world has ever seen, it is not hard to understand how the Moslem would regard his pure monotheism as the very light of heaven. And so it came to pass that, when forty years later (752) the Rajput chiefs succeeded in overthrowing the Moslem power in Sindh, and maintained control for 150 years,[8] the religion of the Moslems continued to spread even beyond the regions once under Mohammedan government. Elliot, in his history of India, tells us of certain Sindhian princes who became Mohammedans at this time, assuming Arab names.[9] By and by the Moslems, reinforced by Karmathian refugees from Egypt, formed independent dynasties at Multan and at Mansura in lower Sindh. Arab travellers, visiting Sindh in the tenth century, reported the presence of Arab chiefs of the Koreish tribe ruling in both the upper and lower provinces. They heard both the Arabic and Sindhi languages spoken and noticed the friendly toleration between the Moslem and Hindu population.

[8] *Mediaeval India*, p. 10.

[9] Elliot's *History of India*, p. 101.

The history of the Mohammedan conquest of India, as recorded by the native historians, has but little to say of the organisation of the religious forces of Islam. These historians have contented themselves with the story of the sultans and their great generals, portraying their triumphs and defeats. These tales of battles fought and won pass before us like a great panorama. The chief pictures in the foreground are those of the heroes of the conquest.

The conquest of Sindh by the Arabs was not the conquest of India by the Moslems. But before we turn to that event, we must follow up the story of the conversion of the Sindhian population to Islam during the interval 752 to 997, during which the Hindus once more held the political supremacy. As we have seen there remained at least two centres of Moslem influence wherein the Mohammedans held sway, Multan and Mansura in Southern Sindh. The Moslems had established their religious institutions and were in correspondence with the Caliphs in the West. They were, however, too weak to undertake any conquests in India. They could with difficulty maintain a semblance of control at home.

And yet it is certain that Islam made inroads upon Hinduism and added many converts to the Moslem faith. Several reasons may be adduced to account for these conversions. First among these reasons was the superiority of the Moslem religion, being a pure monotheism in contrast with the gross idolatry of the Hindu and the fetichism of the outcaste. Another reason lies in the social system of Islam which accords a recognition of equality in the brotherhood, which Hinduism refused to its votaries. It was a deliverer to the downcast *Malaich* or low caste population and many then, as they now do, readily embraced the opportunity of escape by accepting the faith of Islam. Still another influence which operated powerfully to draw over converts from the non-Moslem population was that of relationship. The convert was anxious that his relatives should receive the new religion.

With the Moslems every sort of motive was legitimate in order to advance the faith. Hence permanency of office under the Moslem regime was conditioned upon acceptance of Islam. To secure a tenure upon landed property was possible to him who would accept the new religion. Marriage relationship with a non-Moslem always meant the conversion of the infidel. In every case such voluntary acceptance of the faith meant admission into the rights and privileges enjoyed by every member of the Mohammedan brotherhood. Still farther we should not fail to note that frequently violent feuds among the families and castes of the Hindu population found a ready solution by one of the parties apostatising to Islam. In this way the Moslem community, bound together by a common faith and polity, was ever being increased in numbers and influence, affording security to its own adherents and becoming an ever increasing menace to those outside.

This Arab endeavour to conquer India proved a failure, but it availed to bring under the Moslem banner a multitude which afterward contributed not a little towards that conquest, when undertaken by the Turks and Afghans who poured into India from the northwest.

The first successful attempt to conquer India from the northwest was begun by Sabuktagin the Sultan of Ghazni in Afghanistan. Having twice defeated the Brahman King of the Punjab, whom he made a tributary, he died. His son was the celebrated "Idol-breaker," Sultan Mahmud, lately governor of Khorassan. Mahmud was a devout Moslem, a zealot who yearned for the opportunity to spread the true faith. He was a man of great energy, fearless in battle and ambitious to extend the rule of Islam to the ends of the earth. His faith assured him of rich rewards both for the present world and for that which is to come. Death for himself and for every faithful soldier of the Crescent was but the door to Paradise and a martyr's crown. He set himself to complete the work his father had begun. He vowed he would lead an expedition into India once every year. The first came near to being his last, but the fortunate frightening of the elephant upon which was seated the Hindu Raja Anandpal culminated in a panic and the retreat of the idolaters. Two days of slaughter and pillage brought boundless booty to the hands of the Moslems. The treasure city of Kangra soon fell into the hands of the triumphant army. "Immense stores of treasure and jewels, money and silver ingots, were laden upon camels, and a pavilion of silver and a canopy of Byzantine linen reared upon pillars of silver and gold were among the prizes of the Holy War. The booty was displayed in the court of the palace at Ghazni. Jewels and unbored pearls and rubies, shining like sparks or iced wine, emeralds as it were sprigs of young myrtle, diamonds as big as pomegranates. The eastern chroniclers tell of seventy million silver dirhams, and hundreds of thousand pounds' weight of silver cups and vessels."[10]

With such rich reward, is it wonderful that thousands of Moslem youth from Afghanistan, Persia and Central Asia should float annually to the standards of the great Idol-breaker? Mahmud never seems to have wanted for an army to undertake any of his expeditions. The greed of the robber added to the zeal of the devotee filled the ranks with strong, determined men, who swept everything before them until the very burden of the plunder obliged a return to the fastnesses of Central Asia. Sixteen times between the years 1000 and 1026, he led his Moslem legions into India, ravaging the country now included within the boundaries of the Northwest Frontier Province, the Punjab, the united Provinces of Agra and Oudh and a portion of Central India. The divided state of the country, owing to internal dissensions between the Hindu rajas, made it possible for the Moslems to defeat their enemies in detail. Each expedition added to the hoards of booty stored in Ghazni and enlisted new recruits.

And yet Mahmud did not establish himself on the throne of India. He had a higher ambition. He strove to rule over Central Asia with India as an annex. From the sea of Aral to the banks of the Euphrates and from the Oxus to the Ganges, he ruled as supreme potentate, sending his armies east, west and south to plunder and subdue the uncircumcised. Everywhere he carried the

[10] *Mediaeval India*, p. 21.

sword to kill the infidels and everywhere bestowed the clemency of Moslem rule upon those who submitted to the yoke of Islam. Bloody as were his conquests, Mahmud is still revered by the Moslems of the world as a god-fearing king full of a holy zeal for the faith. He distinguished himself by his relentless iconoclasm. No bribe or prayer ever availed to shield an idol or a heathen temple from destruction. The sack of the temple of Somnath, where fifty thousand Hindus laid down their lives in defence of the famous linga, a stone pillar decorated with gold and jewels to the value of $5,000,000, was his greatest achievement from the religious standpoint. It was, however, typical of many other similar conquests, in which the idols were broken, the temples destroyed and the priests put to death. Multitudes of the miserable people professed the faith of Islam to save their lives or to enter the warrior hosts and receive a share of the plunder. Hindu women and children were enslaved, many becoming the wives and concubines of the conquerors. The great Sultan always said his prayers, as did no doubt the vast majority of the soldiers, before engaging in battle. Thus the spirit of the Moslem invasion was that of a crusade or Holy War, and the purpose was to spread abroad the religion of Islam.

The outcome of these numerous raids into India was the establishment of the Moslem power in the Punjab and Sindh, under a viceroy at Lahore. Elsewhere the Hindu chiefs, although often beaten in battle, were not subdued, so that whenever the Moslem armies evacuated the country, these rajas returned to assume control.

When Mahmud of Ghazni died his son Ma'sud assumed control. Although he was a brave man, a giant in strength, no one being able to wield his battle axe, the great empire rapidly disintegrated and crumbled to pieces. Persia and Khorassan were overrun by Turkish and Turkoman tribes and in 1038 the Seljuk Turk Tughril Beg succeeded in establishing his control over these great provinces. The viceroy at Lahore, Niyaltagin, undertook to become a conqueror, and led an expedition against Benares, where he succeeded in plundering its many temples of a vast amount of booty. Soon after he aspired to become independent, but was defeated. Ma'sud now set himself to retrieve his fortunes in the West but failed. The Seljuks utterly defeated his armies and threatened to attack Ghazni. In despair Ma'sud packed up his treasures and attempted to carry them to India. A rebellion broke out in his army and he was deposed, imprisoned and put to death. From this time and onward for a hundred years the Moslem viceroy and the great Mohammedan chiefs in India practically took care of themselves.

During this period a new dynasty sprang up in Afghanistan, with the great warrior Ghias-ud-din at the head. His brother Muizz-ud-din, known in history as Mohammed Ghori, began a series of raids upon India not unlike those of the great Mahmud of Ghazni. His method, however, looked towards the establishment of an empire. His first step was to bring all the Moslem rulers in India into subjection to himself. He then set himself the task of subduing the Hindus. After suffering a crushing defeat at the hands of the Rajputs under Prithwi Raja, he returned the next year (1192) with 120,000 Afghans, Turks and Persians and after a hard-fought battle at Narain, ten miles north of Karnal and some 75 miles west of Delhi, he utterly defeated the Hindu army and speedily brought the major portion of Rajputana under the Moslem yoke. He then established a viceroyalty with a slave general Kutb-ud-din Aybek in power as viceroy of India. The same year (1192) Kutb-ud-din captured Delhi, where he established the seat of government. A little later a further expedition led by Mohammed Ghori led to the overthrow of the Hindu rajas of Kanauj and Benares and the annexation of their dominions to the empire.

Kutb-ud-din became the king of Delhi upon the death of his master. One of his generals, Mohammed Bakhtiyar Khan, had conquered Oudh and pushing on to Lakhnauti, the capital of Bengal, soon brought the whole of that vast Province under the dominion of the Moslem. The Empire of Ghor, like that of Mahmud of Ghazni, fell to pieces at the death of Mohammed, and the great generals and viceroys set up for themselves. The kingdom of Delhi at the death of the Sultan of Ghor practically extended over the whole of North India. The character of the rule thus imposed upon the millions in North India is thus described by Stanley Lane Poole upon the authority of the Mohammedan historian of the time:

"The viceroy (Kutb-ud-din) administered his wide provinces 'in the ways of justice' and 'the people were happy.' Tribute and military service were exacted as the price of toleration, and Aybek's impartiality is extolled in the metaphorical phrase that 'the wolf and the sheep drank water out of the same pond.' 'The roads were freed from robbers,' and the Hindus, 'both high and low were treated with royal benignity,' which, however, did not prevent the viceroy from making an immense number of slaves in his wars. So munificent was he that he was called the 'Lakhbaksh' or 'giver of lacs.' [11] At Delhi he busied himself in building the great mosque or Jami Masjid and the famous minaret known after his surname as the Kutb Minar, which stood originally two hundred and fifty feet high and is the tallest minaret in the world. Its boldly jutting balconies, alternate angular and rounded fluting, and fine Arabic inscriptions set off the natural contrasts of white marble and red sandstone of which it is built. The mosque, like Aybek's other mosque at Ajmer, was constructed of the materials of demolished temples, and the ornament was supplied from the idols of the Hindus. Aybek was a staunch Moslem, and though policy dictated toleration in the case of powerful Hindu vassals, he was a mighty 'fighter in the way of God.' 'The realm was filled with friends and cleared of foes,' says a contemporary chronicler, 'his bounty was continuous, and so was his slaughter.'" [12]

This account of the character and rule of Delhi's first Mohammedan emperor illustrates the missionary character of Moslem conquest. The government is strictly Moslem in character. Powerful Hindu vassals are tolerated for political reasons. Mosques and pillars, commemorating the victories of the Moslems, are built out

[11] A lac is one hundred thousand rupees.

[12] *Mediaeval India*, pp. 68, 69.

of the stones of demolished temples and broken idols. The whole machinery of government was so constructed as to further the cause of religion. The way to office and emolument was by way of Islam. Immunity from the capitation tax and the political disability of the subject race awaited the man who would walk in "the way of God." The riches and glory of the Kingdom of God on earth beckoned the unbeliever and not in vain. The low caste population in particular found a deliverer in the Moslem ruler. In Bengal, the multitudes of low caste aborigines seem to have welcomed their new rulers and readily to have accepted the new religious faith. The following account of the conversion of a Hindu chief, given us by Professor T. W. Arnold in his very interesting book *The Preaching of Islam,* illustrates another phase of the propagandism. It was when Mahmud of Ghazni arrived near the foot of Barba, the site of the present City of Bulandshahr, that the Hindu chief Hardatta, "hearing of this invasion by the protected warriors of God, who advanced like the waves of the sea, with the angels round them on all sides, became greatly agitated, his steps trembled, and he feared for his life, which was forfeited under the law of God. So he reflected that his safety would best be secured by conforming to the religion of Islam, since God's sword was drawn from the scabbard, and the whip of punishment was uplifted. He came forth therefore, with ten thousand men, who all proclaimed their anxiety for conversion, and their rejection of idols." [13]

A similar course was pursued by many chiefs, adding

[13] Elliot's *History of India,* vol. ii. pp. 42, 43.

much to the military strength of the Moslems. Some of the fiercest opponents to their invasion were the Gakkars, a barbarous tribe in the mountains north of the Punjab. They are said to have been converted by Mohammed Ghori, who having captured a Gakkar chieftain induced him to become a Moslem and then confirming him in his chieftainship sent him back to convert his followers, who having little religion of their own, soon were led to embrace Islam.[14]

This policy of the Mohammedan invaders of India was not only in accord with the law of conquest laid down by their prophet but necessitated by their circumstances. "Their power in India," says Stanley Lane Poole, "was always that of an armed camp, but it was a camp in which all the soldiers fought shoulder to shoulder for the same cause, in which all were equal brothers; and it had the immense resource of being able to draw continually and in unlimited numbers upon the recruiting grounds of the Mohammedan countries behind it, which were always reinforcing their co-religionists by fresh bodies of hardy adventurers free from the lethargy of self-indulgence that too often etiolates the exotic in the Indian forcing house. The very bigotry of their creed was an instrument of self-preservation; in mere self-defence they must hold together as God's elect in the face of the heathen, and they must win over proselytes from the Hindus, whether by persuasion or by the sword, to swell their isolated minority."[15]

[14] This statement is given by Arnold on the authority of Firishta. See *Preaching of Islam*, p. 212.

[15] *Mediaeval India*, p. 63.

In the autobiography of Firoz Shah Tughlak (1351-88) we have the following statement, which indicated the policy if not always the zeal of the Moslem conqueror in India: "I encouraged my infidel subjects to embrace the religion of the Prophet, and I proclaimed that every one who repeated the creed and became a Mussulman should be exempt from the *Jizyah* or poll-tax. Information of this came to the ears of the people at large and great numbers of Hindus presented themselves, and were admitted to the honour of Islam. Thus they came forward day by day from every quarter, and, adopting the faith, were exonerated from the *Jizyah,* and were favoured with presents and honours."[16]

These facts will suffice to show how this wholesale conversion of the people served to strengthen the Moslem power in India. The vast majority of the converts were cultivators of the soil or soon became such. Vast landed estates were parcelled out to chiefs, who encouraged the farmers to become Moslems. The numerous tenants-at-will were able to secure tenant rights and become practically the owners of the lands they cultivated by accepting the religion of the conqueror. Add to this the intermarriage of the soldiers with Hindu women and the forcible conversion of women and children taken captive in war, and it will be seen how rapidly the faith spread in spite of the awful slaughter and bloodshed incident upon almost continual war during a period of more than five hundred years. The clannishness of the Hindus and their jealousy of each other, added to the disintegrating influences of caste, destroyed everything that would inspire the nation with

[16] Elliot, vol. iii. p. 386.

true patriotism. The religion too irrevocably bound up with principles of caste exclusiveness rendered them void of anything like a missionary spirit. The death of the Hindu warrior and the conversion of the Hindu renegade alike served to weaken the forces of the Hindus and to strengthen the cause of Islam.

But for the constant warring of rival claimants to the Moslem throne and the awful scourge of the Mongol robbers under Genghis Khan, which served to weaken the Moslem kingdom and even to threaten its existence, we can hardly see how the Hindu could have maintained his hold upon his religion.

After the death of Kutb-ud-din, his favourite slave, Altamish, imitating his master, set aside the worthless heir to the throne and made himself Sultan and after a stormy career succeeded in defeating his rivals and in overthrowing the Mongol invaders and finally in extending his dominion toward the south by the conquest of Malwa as far as Ujjain. Up to this time no Moslem army had ventured south of the Vindhaya range of mountains. In the year 1294 Ala-ud-din, a daring prince with 8,000 men, forced his way through the mountains and marched 700 miles to attack Devagiri, the capital of the Maratha king. By lying and deceit he managed to secure the submission of the Hindu raja. A few years later, when Ala-ud-din, now Sultan of Delhi, had rid himself of the Mongol invaders, he sent another expedition into the Deccan, under the leadership of a Hindu renegade Malik Kafur, who laid the country waste and brought back the rebel king of Devagiri and his sons to Delhi. Here policy again dictated the conduct of the Sultan, who loaded the Hindu captive raja with honours and a rich present and sent him back to rule his kingdom as his vassal. In the next expedition, this Hindu king sent a contingent of Marathas to aid in the conquest of Warangal in the Eastern Ghats. In 1310 this same army conquered the country on the Malabar Coast as far as Mysore and brought back to Delhi an almost incredible quantity of booty, the gold weighing 1200 tons.

We here see practically the same course of Moslem conquest which has been described in our account of the establishment of Mohammedan power in North India. Without detailing the incidents of rebellion, revolution and anarchy which frequently followed the death of such a tyrant as Ala-ud-din, we will confine our narrative to a few leading men, who brought about the conquest of South India.

In 1321, Mohammed Tughlak was proclaimed by the army. He brought peace and prosperity once more to the empire and reasserted Moslem authority over Bengal and Southern India. At his death a long period of misrule ensued and the empire once more began to disintegrate, and when Timur, in 1398, following in the footsteps of his predecessor Genghis Khan, but with the pious purpose of destroying the infidels and their idols, came into India with his army of 92,000 horsemen, he found the people divided and so unable to resist his furious assault. City after city was destroyed and soon the conqueror found himself at Panipat confronted by the Indian army. After putting to death in cold blood 100,000 Hindu prisoners, Timur said his prayers and ordered an assault. He was everywhere triumphant and soon Delhi was surrendered. After three days of slaughter and rapine the conqueror retired and returned to Samarkand. Timur, like his Moslem predecessors, claimed to be a propagator of the true faith. "My object [said he] in the invasion of Hindustan is to lead a campaign against the infidels, to convert them to the true faith according to the command of Mohammed (on whom and his family be the blessing and peace of God); to purify the land from the defilement of misbelief and polytheism, and overthrow the temples and the idols, whereby we shall be *ghazis* and *mujahids*, champions and soldiers of the faith before God."[17]

The empire was now split up into various sultanates, each extending its authority by bloody warfare and rapine. The Sayyad kings maintained the semblance of Moslem government in Delhi for a few years, but lacked the energy to recover the losses incident upon the destruction wrought by Timur. It remained for another horde of Afghan warriors under the leadership of Bahlol Lodi (1451), to restore in some degree the strength and glory of the former regime. Independent Sultans ruled in Bengal, Oudh, Rajputana, Gujarat and the Deccan, each one of which not only sustained the supremacy of the faith within its own borders but extended that faith among the non-Moslem tribes. Perhaps nothing more clearly proves the marvellous hold of Islam upon the millions of its votaries in India than the existence and strength of the many independent Moslem kingdoms of this period.

[17] *Mediaeval India*, p. 155.

It remained for still another king of Afghanistan to restore to Islam in India that virility necessary to re-establish the Moslem Empire in India. Babar, king of Kabul, having in his veins the blood of both the Mongol and the Turk, possessed the wisdom and the courage to lay the foundation of a new empire. He came at the request of some of the most powerful chiefs in India who desired to end the misrule in Delhi. In two brief but bloody campaigns (1524-25) he led his triumphant army into Delhi and "on Friday, April 26, public prayer was said in the mosque of the capital in the name of the new emperor, the first of the Great Moguls." [18]

The powers of Islam were soon to be confronted by the most formidable army of unbelievers which had ever been arrayed against them. The great Rana Sanga of Chitor, the head of all the Rajput princes, one hundred and twenty in number, led an army of 80,000 horse and 500 elephants to contest the right of the Moslem to rule in Delhi. The pious Babar seemed to realise how much was at stake. Calling his officers together he said: "Gentlemen and soldiers, every man that comes into the world must pass away: God alone is immortal, unchangeable. Whoso sits down to the feast of life must end by drinking the cup of death. All visitors of the inn of mortality must one day leave this house of sorrow. Rather let us die with honour than live disgraced.

"With fame, though I die, I am content,
Let fame be mine, though life be spent.

"God most high has been gracious in giving us this

[18] *Mediaeval India*, p. 203.

destiny, that if we fall we die martyrs, if we conquer we triumph in his holy cause. Let us swear with one accord by the great name of God that we will never turn back from such a death, or shrink from the stress of battle, till our souls are parted from our bodies."

"The response was enthusiastic. Every man seized the Quran and took the oath." [19] A bloody battle ensued which resulted in the destruction of the Hindu army.

This incident in the history of the Mogul Empire is here given to show that while Moslem contended with Moslem for dominion, all alike regarded war with idolaters as a holy war and its end the triumph of Islam. It was during the period 1525-1707, when the power of the Moguls became established throughout India, that the religion of Islam made its most brilliant and extended conquests. The names of Akbar, Jahangir, Shah Jehan and Aurangzeb occupy the chief places in the galaxy of Mogul emperors. They most of all encouraged literature and the fine arts. To them we owe those monuments in stone and marble, of which Moslems may well be proud and which still lend so much lustre to Mohammedan rule in India. And yet it is to be doubted whether Islam did not at this time receive a serious check in the empire. The tolerance of Akbar, who not only removed the poll-tax (*Jizyah*) from all his non-Moslem subjects, but who established a sort of parliament of religions, inviting Brahmans, Persian Sufis, Parsi fire worshippers and Jesuit priests to freely discuss in his presence the special tenets of their faith and practice. He went further and promul-

[19] *Mediaeval India*, p. 208.

gated an eclectic creed of his own and constituted himself a sort of priest king in which his own dictum should override everything excepting the letter of the Quran. His own creed is set forth in the following words of India's greatest poet Abul Fazl:

"O God, in every temple, I see those who see thee, and in every tongue that is spoken, thou art praised.
Polytheism and Islam grope after thee,
Each religion says, 'Thou art one, without equal,'
Be it mosque, men murmur holy prayer; or church, the bells ring, for love of thee.
Awhile I frequent the Christian cloister, anon the mosque:
But thee only I seek from fane to fane.
Thine elect know naught of heresy or orthodoxy, whereof neither stands behind the screen of thy truth
Heresy to the heretic,—dogma to the orthodoxy,—
But the dust of the rose-petal belongs to the heart of the perfume-seller."

It is said that Akbar's new eclectic religion degenerated into a sort of "eclectic pantheism," which in the eyes of the orthodox Moslem is idolatry. But few adopted it. Still the effect of Akbar's innovations tended to corrupt the people who had adopted a pure monotheism. Shrines in honour of Moslem saints were set up all over the country and were the scene of votive offerings made by both Moslems and Hindus. To him are traced the many idolatrous ceremonies and practices still common among the Indian Moslems.

After the death of Shah Jehan, the emperor Aurangzeb undertook to reform the religion of the empire. He abolished the law which exonerated the idolaters from the payment of poll-tax and brought them under the law of the Quran. With fire and sword he entered upon a crusade against the idols. The idolaters were slain or forcibly obliged to accept Islam. The result was the awakening of every hostile influence and the arraying of the non-Moslem population against the tyranny of the ruling despot. At the death of Aurangzeb, the political power of the Mohammedans began to wane. The Sikhs eventually secured control in the Punjab. The Marathas in the West and South so far secured the upper hand that the emperors in Delhi became their puppets, and but for the incoming of the English, it is probable that the Mohammedan empire would have been wiped out. The conquest of India by the English brought to all classes religious liberty. Under the peaceful rule of the Christians, Islam is enabled to reorganise its forces and propagate its tenets among the people without let or hindrance.

The progress which the religion of Islam has made in India during its twelve centuries of conquest and missionary effort may be seen by reference to the Census Report for the year 1902. This report shows that the total Moslem population in the Indian Empire aggregates 62,458,077, which is more than one-fifth of the total population, of which about 50,000,000 belong to Northern India:

From a political standpoint Islam has lost its power in India, but under the new conditions, it remains to be seen what missionary zeal and influence it is able to arouse amongst its adherents and what conquests it is capable of making without the aid of the proselyting sword. It is just here where its real spiritual conflict with Christianity begins. It is just here where the Christian Church must seek her way to victory. Carnal weapons she has used more than once, but with carnal weapons she has not brought the followers of Islam into subjection to her Gospel. Only by her spiritual equipment may she hope to succeed. Only when the Moslem comes to see Allah as He is revealed to mankind in Jesus the Messiah, will he joyfully cry with converted Thomas, "My Lord and my God."

III

MOSLEM CONQUEST IN THE FAR EAST

We have already considered in some measure the missionary forces, which operated along with the power of the sword, to establish and propagate the religion of Islam in India. Much more might have been said to illustrate the influence of the mullahs and dervishes who poured into India from Arabia, Egypt, Central Asia and Persia. Much might have been told of the influence of Moslem merchants and traders, who have been from the beginning a special agency for the propagation of Islam in all parts of the Eastern world.

We are now to turn our attention to regions wherein Islam has been propagated by more peaceful methods, and where the sword has had comparatively little to do as a proselyting agency.[1]

The countries into which Islam was carried by methods which we will call missionary to distinguish them from the methods of a military crusade, are Thibet, Northern China and the Islands of Malaysia or the East Indian Archipelago. These countries, at

[1] We are indebted to Professor T. W. Arnold, late Principal of the Government College, Lahore, for preparing with prodigious labour that most interesting account of the propagation of the Moslem faith which he has presented to English readers in his treatise entitled *The Preaching of Islam.*

the time of the rise of Islam, were wholly given over to idolatry. Christianity had made little or no effort to evangelise these peoples, and even Buddhism had done little to obliterate their idolatry, having been satisfied with a national recognition of Buddha as a religious teacher. For centuries preceding the advent of Mohammed the Arabs had extensive mercantile interests in India and the East Indian Archipelago, and even in China, bringing thence the precious stones, gold, silver, spices and costly silks, which were carried by sea to the Persian Gulf and to Alexandria for transmission to Europe.[2] When Arabia accepted the religion of the prophet of Mecca and its people poured forth to propagate the new faith, it was not only possible, but in every way most natural, that her army of merchants should endeavour to propagate their faith in every country into which their business would carry them. It is easy also to understand how, when the great empires of the Moslems were established, these traders would carry with them a dignity and influence which would greatly increase their influence as religious propagandists. As a matter of fact the testimony of both Moslem and Christian writers points to the Arab trader as the pioneer of Moslem missionary endeavour in these Far Eastern dominions. Whenever a number of people became adherents to the new religion, the need of some one to instruct them became apparent and was readily supplied from some centre of Moslem influence, from Arabia or Bagdad, from Persia or India. Every such company of believers was a brotherhood, bound together by a common

[2] Niemann's *Inleiding Tot de Kennis van den Islam*, p. 337.

faith and a common interest, sometimes culminating in a political influence which eventually conferred upon them supreme dignity. Proceeding now to consider in detail the working out of this method of propagating the Mohammedan religion in the Far East, we will begin with China.

Our principal authorities on this subject are Marco Polo and Ibn Batuta of the thirteenth and fourteenth centuries respectively; a Russian writer, Vasil'ev (1867), and a French author, the late Consul General M. P. Dubry de Thiersant (1880), who have made an exhaustive study of the historical literature found in China relating to the Moslems. To these may be added the more recent writings in the Journal of the Asiatic Society, Bengal, and the Journal of the Moslem Institute, of Rai Surat Chandra Das, C. I. E., a gentleman who has made a special study of Thibetan and Chinese literature.

There is a tradition, mentioned by M. de Thiersant, to the effect that when Mohammed in the 6th year of the Hegira sent messengers to the various rulers of the earth, he sent Wahab Ibn Abi Kabshah with a letter and suitable presents to the emperor of China asking him to accept the new religion. The emperor is said to have received him kindly and to have given him permission to build a mosque in the city of Canton and the right to propagate this new religion. When this ambassador returned to Medina, it was to learn with sorrow that his Prophet was dead. However, after a year or more Wahab returned to China, taking with him a copy of the Quran, but on his arrival in Canton he was taken ill and died. His tomb is still held in reverence by Chinese Moslems. Bretschneider, in his work on the knowledge possessed by the ancient Chinese of the Arabs and Arabian colonies (London, 1871), says that early in the T'ang Dynasty (618-905) reference is made in the Chinese annals, to the arrival in Canton of "A great number of strangers from the Kingdom of Annam, Cambodia, Medina and several other countries." Of these strangers it is said that "they worshipped the heaven (*i. e.* God), and had neither statue, idol nor image in their temples. The kingdom of Medina is close to India: in this kingdom originated the religion of these strangers, which is different from that of Buddha. They do not eat pork or drink wine, and they regard as unclean the flesh of any animal not killed by themselves.[3] They are nowadays called Hoi-Hoi (Hui-Hui). They had a temple, called the Temple of Blessed Memory, which was built at the commencement of the T'ang Dynasty. At the side of the temple is a large round tower, 160 feet high, called Kang-ta (the undecorated tower). These strangers went every day to this temple to perform their ceremonies. . . . they were very rich and obeyed a chief chosen by themselves." [4]

There can be no doubt that these "strangers" or foreigners were Arab merchants, who professed the Mohammedan faith and who had a mosque at this centre. Of these, as of others elsewhere, it is said that they

[3] Alluding to the Moslem custom of killing in the name of God, so rendering the flesh *halál* or lawful.

[4] M. De Thiersant, vol. i. pp. 19, 20.

took to themselves Chinese women as wives and so formed an Arab colony in the city. Year by year new arrivals from Arabia and converts drawn from the relatives of their wives were added to their number. The favourable reception of these Arab merchants by the Chinese authorities no doubt greatly promoted the trade between the two great empires. Not only by sea between the Persian Gulf and Canton but also, and especially, in the north, trade was carried on by caravans on the overland route through Central Asia. Mr. Williams, in *The Middle Kingdom,* says, "They formed a large portion of the caravans which went to and fro through Central Asia, and seem to have been received without resistance, if not without favour, until they grew by natural increase to be a large and an integral part of the population."

In 758 the Chinese Arabs received a large accession to their numbers, by the importation of an Arab army, "sent by the Caliph Al-Mansur to aid the Emperor Sah-Tsung in crushing a rebellion that had broken out against him."[5] When the war was over, these soldiers declined to return whence they came; and when an effort was made to compel them to leave, they joined their co-religionists, plundered the principal merchants of the city and obliged the governor to take refuge in his citadel. The governor then reconsidered his position and yielded to the request of the Arabs, assigned them lands and houses, and so made them citizens of the Chinese commonwealth. The soldiers married Chinese women, in some measure adopted Chinese customs, and became the nucleus of a large Moslem population. Simi-

[5] *Preaching of Islam,* p. 251.

lar accessions were made later on at the time of the Mongol conquests under Genghis Khan. The first mosque was built in the capital city of the province of Shen-si about the year 742 A. D. and a special officer was appointed over the affairs of the Moslems. Following upon the devastating wars of Genghis Khan, a great multitude of Moslems, Syrians, Arabs, Persians and others poured into China. "Some came as merchants, artisans, soldiers and colonists, others were brought in as prisoners of war. A great number of them settled in the country and developed into a populous and flourishing community, gradually losing their racial peculiarities by their marriage with Chinese women."[6]

We learn from this meagre account as to the course of Moslem occupation at least this much, that the Arab merchants and Moslem colonists formed in the chief cities separate quarters in which they built mosques modelled after the fashion of Chinese temples. They also adapted themselves to Chinese customs, which would in some measure be due to the Chinese women, who now formed at least one-half the Moslem community. This same accommodation to national customs is seen in India, in Malaysia and in Africa. The essential element in their religious life was the worship of no god but Allah, and even in this they adopted the Chinese names *The-yan-nu* (Lord of Heaven) or simply *The-han* or more simply *Chu* (Lord).[7] They observed prayer, and the tenets of the Quran as to clean and unclean, etc. Many of the Moslems were permitted to occupy high

[6] T. W. Arnold in *Preaching of Islam*, pp. 247, 248.
[7] *Asiatic Journal*, vol. xli.

places in the government provided they had passed the required examinations. The great defect in the education of Chinese Moslems was, and still is, that Arabic was not generally taught, and for this reason their religion maintains the character of a traditional or ancestral religion. The vast majority of the Mohammedan population are ignorant of the faith they profess.

After the expulsion of the Mongol dynasty about the beginning of the fourteenth century, the Chinese Moslems were cut off from their co-religionists. They had come under suspicion of being allied to the hated Mongols, and judging from the number who had held high offices under that dynasty, the accusation was not without reason. They were wiser than the Catholic Christians who lived three centuries later, and, by adapting themselves to the changed conditions, averted destruction. Indeed, they have so completely adapted themselves to Chinese customs that it is difficult for an ordinary observer to distinguish the Moslem from the Buddhist, Taoist or Confucian.[8] "They wear the cue and the ordinary dress of the Chinese, and put on a turban as a rule only in the mosque. To avoid offending a superstitious prejudice on the part of the Chinese,

[8] M. Elisée Reclus in his work, *The Earth and its Inhabitants*, says: "Mohammedans in China can always be distinguished from the other natives by their haughty bearing, frank expression; and in the West, by the practice of carrying arms. Abstaining from alcoholic drinks, tobacco and opium, they are generally more healthy than their neighbours, while their spirit of clanship insures for them a material prosperity far superior to that of the surrounding population."

they also refrain from building tall minarets. Even in Chinese Tartary, where the special privilege is allowed to the Mussulman soldiers of forming a separate body, the higher Mohammedan officials wear the dress prescribed to their rank, long moustaches and the cue, and on holidays they perform the usual homage demanded from officials to a portrait of the emperor, by touching the ground three times with their forehead. Similarly all Mohammedan mandarins and other officials in other provinces perform the rites prescribed to their official position, in the temple of Confucius on festival days. In fact every precaution is taken by the Moslems to prevent their faith from appearing to be in opposition to the state religion, and hereby they have succeeded in avoiding the odium with which the adherents of foreign religions, such as Judaism and Christianity, are regarded. They even represent their religion to their Chinese fellow-countrymen as being in agreement with the teachings of Confucius, with only this difference, that they follow the traditions of their ancestors with regard to marriages, funerals, the prohibition of pork, wine, tobacco and games of chance, and the washing of hands before meals. Similarly the writings of the Chinese Mohammedans treat the works of Confucius and other Chinese classics with great respect, and when possible, point out the harmony between the teachings continued therein and the doctrines of Islam." [9]

Under conditions like these, it is not surprising to

[9] T. W. Arnold in *Preaching of Islam*, on authority Vasil'ev, pp 15, 16. Vambery Trooso in *Central Asia*, p. 404, and De Thiersant, vol. i. pp. 367, 372.

learn that the Chinese government has been tolerant of the Hoi-Hois, inasmuch as they appear to be but one of the numerous sects, which having doctrines and customs peculiar to itself yet recognises a formal allegiance to the national faith and state religion. This circumstance also renders it difficult to arrive at definite information in regard to the Moslem population in China. Upon this subject we find a great variety of opinion.

In the year 1889 the venerable Dr. Happer of Canton wrote me a private letter on this point, as follows: "As to the number of Moslems in China, we have no reliable information. They are resident largely in two provinces, the northwest and southwest ones. Some twenty years ago they broke out in rebellion and the internal war was continued for twenty years, resulting in great loss of life, and a large diminution of the Moslems. They generally conform to the Chinese usages to such a degree that they suffer no disabilities. There are few in the South." Again in a notice of M. de Thiersant's book, the same writer says: "M. de Thiersant, Consul General of France, in his book on *Mohametisme en Chine,* etc., gives the number of the Mohammedan population in China as twenty millions, as quoted in the *Edinburgh Review* for April, 1880, on page 368. He gives the number for each province with the utmost minutiæ. Every one acquainted with the character of the Chinese population must regard this statement of the number of Mohammedans in this empire as exaggerated. As the Consul General does not give his authorities for the statement, or the grounds on which he makes the statement, it is difficult, of course, to investigate the matter. But there are some facts patent to all that will help us in forming an opinion. The Moslem population is located largely in three provinces, in Yun-nan in the southwest, and in the adjoining provinces of Kan-suh and Shen-si in the northwest. To Kan-suh 8,350,000 are assigned, 6,500,000 to Shen-si, and 4,000,000 to Yun-nan. As the population of Kan-suh, according to the census of 1872, was 15,193,125, if the Moslems were as stated above, it would make them more than one-half the population. The population of Shen-si at that time was 10,207,256; if the number of Mohammedans was as above given, it would make the Moslems more than six-tenths of the population. The population of Yun-nan in 1872 was 5,561,320; if four millions were Mohammedan before the late rebellion, that class of the people would have been nearly four-fifths of the entire population. As it is stated that the Moslems were nearly exterminated, it is incredible that four-fifths could have been exterminated by one-fifth. It is a much more plausible supposition that the Moslems were less than one-half of the population, say two millions. The protraction of the war for nineteen years shows that the parties were scarcely of equal numbers, but that the majority were of the party that finally prevailed. We think that the numbers assigned to Kan-suh and Shen-si must be much less than the number above stated, probably less than one-half the number. It is probable that the whole number of Mohammedans in the empire does not exceed three millions."

Mr. A. H. Keane, in *Asia*, edited by Sir Richard Temple, p. 578, puts the Moslem population of the Chinese Empire at thirty millions. Surat Chandra Das estimates it at fifty millions and Sayyad Sulayman, a prominent Moslem officer in the Province of Yun-nan, declares there are now seventy million Moslems in China. These extremes of opinion (for the absence of any reliable statistics is admitted), suggest that the judgment of M. de Thiersant, who made careful inquiry and secured his data from Chinese officials, is on the whole, at least approximately correct.

An important lesson to be drawn from these statistics by every missionary is that we have here an object lesson on the expansive character of Islam, which should be most carefully considered. The old idea that Islam can be propagated only by the sword or by political influence must be abandoned. The fact of a Moslem community of twenty millions of people in China, capable of maintaining a sanguinary war against the government during a period of twenty years, costing the sacrifice of two millions of lives, is sufficiently important to assure us that we have in the Hoi-Hois of China a body of men whose influence in the evangelisation of China cannot be ignored. This body has gathered within its fold the remnants of Judaism and Nestorian Christianity found in China by Marco Polo in the thirteenth century.[10] It has been absolutely untouched by Roman Catholicism. Only a pure Christianity can hope to win this multitude, which has stood as a witness for monotheism amid the countless millions of idolaters in China for more than a thousand years.

[10] Yule's *Marco Polo*, vol. i. p. 141 and vol. ii. p. 39.

We will close this account of Moslem progress in China, by a paragraph from Arnold's *Preaching of Islam,* p. 257, showing the energy and strength of the modern Moslem propaganda in China. "In the towns, the Mohammedans tend little by little to form separate Mohammedan quarters, and finally do not allow any person to dwell among them who does not go to the mosque.[11] Islam has also gained ground in China, because of the promptitude with which the Mohammedans have repeopled provinces devastated by the various scourges so familiar to China. In times of famine they purchase children from poor parents, bring them up in the faith of Islam, and when they are full-grown, provide them with wives and houses, often forming whole villages of these new converts. In the famine that devastated the province of Kwangtung in 1790, as many as 10,000 children are said to have been purchased in this way from parents who, too poor to support them, were compelled by necessity to part with their starving little ones.[12] Sayyad Sulayman says that the number of accessions to Islam gained in this way every year is beyond counting. Every effort is made to keep faith alive among the new converts, even the humblest being taught, by means of metrical primers, the fundamental doctrines of Islam. To the influence of the religious books of the Chinese Moslems, Sayyad Sulayman attributes many of the conversions that are made at the

[11] L'Abbé Grosier, *De la Chine,* etc., tome iv. p. 508.

[12] John Anderson, *Chinese Mohammedans* (*Journal Anthropological Institute of Great Britain and Ireland,* vol. i. p. 151).

present day.[13] Thus, though they have no organised propaganda, yet the zealous spirit of proselytism with which the Chinese Mussulmans are animated, secures for them a constant succession of new converts, and they confidently look forward to the day when Islam will be triumphant throughout the length and breadth of the Chinese Empire."

We now turn to the question of the introduction and propagation of Islam in the Malay Archipelago. All writers are agreed that the first missionaries to these islands were Arab traders, who had in great measure controlled the trade in the eastern seas from the second century B. C., and onward until the advent of the Portuguese.[14] We have already made mention of the mercantile colonies in China, and have seen how they formed a nucleus for the rapid extension of Islam in that Empire. The following extract from Semper's *Die Philippinen und ihre Bewöhner,* quoted by Arnold, in which we have a description of the methods adopted by these merchant missionaries, will illustrate their methods of propagating Islam elsewhere: "The better to introduce their religion into the country, the Mohammedans adopted the language and many of the customs of the natives, married their women, purchased slaves in order to increase their personal importance, and succeeded finally in incorporating themselves among the chiefs who held the foremost rank in the state. Since

[13] *Thamarat-ul-Funun* (17th Shawal, p. 3) and W. J. Smith's *Present Phases of the Mohammedan Question* (*The Churchman,* London, January, 1888, and De Thiersant, tome I. p. 39.)

[14] Niemann, *Inleiding Tot de Kennis van den Islam,* p. 337.

they worked together with greater ability and harmony than the natives, they gradually increased their power more and more, and having numbers of slaves in their possession, they formed a kind of confederacy among themselves and established a sort of monarchy, which they made hereditary in one family. Though such a confederacy gave them great power, yet they felt the necessity of keeping on friendly terms with the old aristocracy, and of ensuring their freedom to those classes whose support they could not afford to dispense with." [15]

This it seems was the general policy pursued throughout the Islands.

The point in the Malay Islands nearest to the seat of Islam was the northern point of Sumatra. Moslem history informs us that here in the land of Atjih, the first company of Moslem missionaries (merchants) began their work. Mention is made of two leaders, Sheikh Abdullah Arif and Jahan Shah. The latter seems to have been an immigrant from the west, and by his influence became so popular among the people that he was proclaimed king under the half Sanscrit, half Arabic title of Sri Paduka Sultan.

This movement does not seem to have gained much headway because Marco Polo makes no mention of it, though he had spent five months in Atjih in 1292. He said all were idolaters excepting the inhabitants of the petty kingdom Parlak in the northwest corner of the island. In 1507-1522, the king of Atjih, Ali Mughayyat Shah, embraced the Moslem faith. It is indeed probable that Islam had been making quiet progress

[15] Arnold's *Preaching of Islam*, p. 295.

among the heathen for some time. Ibn Batuta (tome iv., pp. 230-6) makes mention of a king Maliku'z-Zahir, who was reigning in Samudra in 1345. He is represented as being in touch with the Moslem powers in the west. Many of his advisers were Persians, who probably came from India, and ambassadors were sent to the court at Delhi. His dominion extended for hundreds of miles along the coast and it is expressly said that he was a great general who made war upon the heathen of the surrounding country until they submitted to his rule and paid tribute.[16] Let it not be forgotten, that Islam, however it may be introduced, seizes the first opportunity to use the secular power to further its conquests. The constant struggle of the Dutch to overcome and keep in subjection the descendants of these Acheen Moslems testifies to the military character of these warriors of northern Sumatra. The blood of the sons of Ishmael still courses in their veins and makes the Acheenese the sturdiest champions of Islam and the bitterest foes of the Christian rulers in Malaysia. But for the advent of the Christian traders, Portuguese, Spanish and Dutch, it is probable that the whole population of the island if not of the entire Archipelago would have become Moslem.

It was early in the last century (1803) when three pilgrims from Sumatra, falling in with the Wahabi movement at Mecca, returned home full of zeal to reform Islam in their native land. They began preaching a crusade against the worship of saints, drinking and

[16] Ibn Batuta, tome iv. pp. 230-6, as reported by Arnold, p. 297.

gambling and other abuses in the religion of Islam. Gathering a number of followers they proclaimed a *Jihad* or holy war against the heathen Battas, which soon became a savage and bloody war. In 1821 these zealots came in contact with the Dutch and a long war ensued, lasting seventeen years, when their last stronghold was taken. But it must not be supposed that Islam has ceased to make converts from the heathen Batta tribes. Each year marks the inroads of the Moslem as well as of the Christian and it is only a question of time when they will be absorbed by these two rival religions.

The introduction of Islam into the Malay peninsula, lying east of Sumatra, may have been as early as the time already alluded to when Arab merchants visited Sumatra, Java and other islands of the Archipelago. But the establishment of the religion in the north of Sumatra opened a way of easy access to the Island of Singapore and thence to the Peninsula. Moslem annals tell us of the powerful Kingdom of Menangkabau on the east coast of Sumatra, which first sent its missionaries to the neighbouring islands and to the Peninsula. These were the forerunners of adventurers who set up for themselves principalities, whose chiefs still receive their investiture from that place.[17] We read of a certain Mohammed Shah who reigned as Sultan of Malacca in the end of the thirteenth century. De Barras, a Portuguese historian, tells of an Arabian Cadi who came to Malacca in 1388 and having converted the king gave him the name of Mohammed Shah.[18] It

[17] *Preaching of Islam*, p. 300. [18] *Idem*, p. 300, note.

was in the beginning of the sixteenth century when the Kingdom of Queda became Mohammedan. The story of this event as recorded in the annals of Queda is exceedingly suggestive as to the missionary methods of that time. We give it as reported by Mr. Arnold.

"A learned Arab, by name Sheikh Abdullah, having come to Queda, visited the Raja and inquired what was the religion of the country. 'My religion,' replied the Raja, 'and that of all my subjects is that which has been handed down to us by the people of old. We all worship idols.' 'Then has your highness never heard of Islam, and of the Quran which descended from God to Mohammed, and has superseded all other religions, leaving them in the possession of the devil?' 'I pray you then if this be true,' said the Raja, 'to instruct and enlighten us in this new faith.' In a transport of holy fervour at this request Sheikh Abdullah embraced the Raja and then instructed him in the creed. Persuaded by his teaching, the Raja sent for all his jars of spirits (to which he was much addicted), and with his own hands emptied them on the ground. After this he had all the idols of the palace brought out; the idols of gold, and silver, and clay and wood, were all heaped up in his presence, and were all broken and cut in pieces by Sheikh Abdullah with his sword and with an axe, and the fragments consumed in the fire.

"The Sheikh asked the Raja to assemble all his women of the fort and palace. When they had all come into the presence of the Raja and the Sheikh, they were initiated into the doctrines of Islam. The Sheikh was mild and courteous in his demeanour, persuasive and soft in his language, so that he gained the hearts of the inmates of the palace.

"The Raja soon after sent for the four aged ministers, who on entering the hall, were surprised at seeing a Sheikh seated near the Raja. The Raja explained to them the object of the Sheikh's coming; whereupon the four chiefs expressed their readiness to follow the example of his Highness, saying, 'We hope that Sheikh Abdullah will instruct us also.' The latter hearing these words, embraced the four ministers and said that he hoped that, to prove their sincerity, they would send for all the people to come to the audience hall, bringing with them all the idols that they were wont to worship and the idols that had been handed down by the men of former days. The request was complied with and all the idols kept by the people were at that very time brought down and there destroyed and burnt to dust; no one was sorry at this demolition of their false gods, all were glad to enter the pale of Islam."

The name of the king was then changed to Sultan Muzlaful Shah instead of the old name of Pra Ang Mahawangsa. As the head of the Moslem community he built mosques in the larger towns and ordered drums to be beaten to call the people to prayer on Friday. The missionary Sheikh Abdullah instructed the people, who flocked in from all parts of the country to be initiated into the rites of the new faith.[19]

[19] *Preaching of Islam*, pp. 301, 302 and *Keddah Annals* by Lieutenant-Colonel James Law, vol. iii pp. 474-477.

This story reveals to us very clearly the relation of the Arab missionary to his converts. He came to them as a friend. He visited the king first of all, setting before him the excellency of the new religion. We know little as to the line of argument used to convert the king. Whether any worldly motives, such as the perpetuity of his dominion guaranteed by the powerful Arab empires in the west, or immunity from the Moslem marauders of Sumatra, were used we know not. We know that the new convert became zealous in the propagation of the faith. The story reminds one of the sudden conversion to the Christian faith of some of the kings and nobles of Scandinavia or of the more recent conversion of the King of Uganda.

Islam was introduced into Java by Arab traders, who as merchant missionaries everywhere invited the people to embrace the new religion. This was in accord with the exhortation of Mohammed who said, "Who speaketh better than he who inviteth unto God, and worketh righteousness and saith, I am a Moslem." (Quran Chap. xli. 33).

The conditions in Java were unique in the history of Moslem propagandism in Malaysia.

Here there was no conquering host and therefore no Moslem state to give dignity and strength to the new religion. The country was in the hands of Hindus and a Hindu civilisation had raised the people above those of the neighbouring islands in culture and progress. The work of propagating the faith was slow and it was only after centuries that the number of Moslems became sufficiently great to attract attention. The methods adopted were those mentioned before: colonisation, marrying native women and conversion of relatives to the faith of Mohammed. After a time, a scion of Hindu royalty in the eastern end of the island, who had been converted to Islam, planned the overthrow of the Hindu kingdom of Mahapahit. He was successful and in 1478 he set up a Moslem kingdom instead. From this time and onward the struggle for supremacy continued until about the middle of the sixteenth century, when they became supreme throughout the Island.

The Arab merchants and Moslem traders in Sumatra and Java migrated into the Moluccas at an early period, but little is known concerning the progress of Islam in these islands before the advent of the Portuguese and Spaniards in the beginning of the sixteenth century. In the fifteenth century the chief of Tidor came under the influence of an Arab trader named Sheikh Mansur and became a Moslem with many of his followers. About the same time, or possibly a few years previous, the King of Ternate became a Mohammedan. When the Portuguese conquered these islands they drove out the Mohammedan teachers and undertook to Christianise the people, and for a while they seemed to succeed; but unfortunately the introduction of a foreign domination served to estrange the people so that when the Portuguese were weakened by domestic troubles in the latter half of the sixteenth century the Moslem teachers returned and drew over many who had accepted Christianity. When later the Dutch expelled the Catholic priests the fate of the Christian mission was sealed. The Jesuit missionaries carried off the remaining Christians of Ternate to the Philippines, where their descendants are still to be found in the province of Cavité in the island of Luzon.[20]

From Ternate and Tidor Islam has spread throughout the Moluccas. The facility with which the heathen are converted to Islam, when once Moslem rule is established, is illustrated by the case of these islands. The heathen inhabitants of the interior were called Alfurs. "In modern times," says Arnold, "the existence of certain regulations, devised for the benefit of the state religion, has facilitated to some extent the progress of the Mohammedan religion among the Alfurs of the mainland, *e. g.* . . . any of the Alfur women who marry Mohammedans must embrace the faith of their husbands; offences against the law may be atoned for by conversion to Islam; and in filling up any vacancy that may happen to occur among the chiefs, less regard is paid to the lawful claims of a candidate than to his readiness to become a Mussulman." [21]

This incident shows how political influence is made to do duty in the absence of the proselyting sword. The introduction of Islam into the Island of Borneo emphasises the same policy. The people of the petty kingdom of Banjarmasin asked the help of one of the Moslem states to suppress a revolt. The help was given on condition that they should profess the faith of Islam. The condition was accepted and thereupon a body of Moslem warriors went over from Java and suppressed the revolt and constituted Banjarmasin a

[20] Crawfurd's *Descriptive History*, p. 85.
[21] Arnold, *Preaching of Islam*, p. 316.

Moslem kingdom. When the Spaniards reached Borneo in 1521 they found another Moslem kingdom at Brunai. In 1550 Arab traders introduced their religion into the western part of the Island. Oliver de Noort in his history tells us of his visit to Borneo in 1660 and that he found the religion of Islam generally professed in the coast towns, while the savages in the interior were all idolaters.[22] Later on one of the inland tribes professed Islam. It was the tribe of the Idaans which seems to have been drawn toward Islam by the superior knowledge which the Moslems had in regard to God and the future life. If so we have here another illustration of the way in which ignorant savages are influenced by the monotheism of the Mohammedans.

In the conversion of the native tribes of the Celebes we have still another illustration of the motives which may determine the religious caste of a people for possibly long periods. As a result of Catholic and Moslem teaching in the island, the people of Macassar left off their idolatry. They sent messengers to both the Christians and the Moslems asking for teachers, determined to follow the leading of those who should first come. "The Portuguese had hitherto been esteemed zealous enough for their religion, but it seems that Don Ruis Perero, who was then governor of Malacca, was a little deficient in his concern for the faith, since he made a great and very unnecessary delay in sending the priests that were desired. On the other hand, the Queen of Acheen, being a furious Mohammedan, no sooner received an account of this disposition in the people of the island of the Celebes than she immediately dis-

[22] *Histoire generale des voyages*, vol. xiv. p. 225.

patched a vessel full of doctors of the law, who in a short time established their religion effectually among the inhabitants. Some time after came the Christian priests, and inveighed bitterly against the law of Mohammed, but to no purpose; the people of the Celebes had made their choice and there was no possibility of bringing them to alter it. One of the kings of the Island indeed, who had before embraced Christianity, persisted in his faith and most of his subjects were converted to it, but still the bulk of the people of the Celebes continued Mohammedans and are so to this day, and the greatest zealots for their religion of any in the Indies." [23]

There is a moral in this story for the Protestant Christians of the world. Many tribes are giving up their idols and asking for a new religion. Some are holding out their hands towards the Christian Church. What will be the result? If Christianity cannot rise quickly and enter in, then Islam will do so. Indeed it is said that in the end of the seventeenth century the inhabitants of the little kingdom of Balaang-Mongondou in the northern peninsula, who had largely been influenced by Catholic Christians, were won over to Islam by the zeal of the Moslem missionaries. The Chronicler remarks: "The Christians, whose knowledge of the doctrines of their religion was very slight and whose faith was weak, were ill prepared with the weapons of controversy to meet the attacks of the rival creed. Despised by the Dutch Government (1830-

[23] *Preaching of Islam*, p. 320, on authority of John Harris's *History of the Portuguese Empire*, vol. i p. 682.

1844), neglected and well nigh abandoned by the authorities of the Church, they began to look on these foreigners, some of whom had settled among them, as their friends."[24] And so it came to pass that the entire community abandoned Christianity and accepted Islam. About one-half the population has professed Islam—the remainder being idolaters. The Moslems are busily at work among them and among the neighbouring islands of Sambawa, Tambok and Flores, and unless Christian missionaries enter in soon it will only be a question of a few years' time when all these idolaters shall be absorbed by the Moslems.

It remains for us to turn to the Philippine Islands, where Islam has come in contact with American nationality. It is believed that we have here not less than a quarter of a million Moslems who may become citizens of America's most distant colony. These reside in the island of Mindanao and the group of small islands known as the Sulu Islands. It is uncertain when Islam was first introduced. Captain Thomas Forrest, writing in 1775, tells us that the Arabs came to the Island of Mindanao three hundred years before and that the tomb of the first Arab, a Sherif from Mecca, was still shown—"a rude heap of coral rock stones."[25] The Spaniards who came to the Philippines in the early part of the sixteenth century found these islands occupied by Moslem tribes which were more civilised than their neighbours in the North, and successfully resisted

[24] Arnold, *Preaching of Islam*, pp. 321-323.

[25] Quoted from *A Voyage to New Guinea and the Moluccas*, by T. Forrest, pp. 201, 313, by Mr. Arnold in *Preaching of Islam*, p. 324, note.

the efforts of the Spaniards to convert them to Catholic Christianity. The special reason assigned by Professor Arnold to account for the intense hatred of the Spanish rulers by the Moslems is that to submit to the Spaniard meant the sacrifice of his liberty and subjection to avaricious and rapacious priests. In regard to the Moslems in the Sulus he remarks: "The people of Sulu are far from being rigid Mohammedans, indeed the influence of the numerous Christian slaves that they carry off from the Philippines in their predatory excursions is so great that it has even been asserted that they would long ere this have become professed Christians but for the prescience that such a change, by inviting a predominating influence in its priesthood, would inevitably undermine their own authority, and pave the way to the transfer of their dominions to the Spanish yoke, an occurrence which fatal experience has too forcibly instructed all the surrounding nations that unwarily embrace the Christian persuasion." [26]

It would seem that the presence of Catholic missionaries in the Sulu Islands has aroused violent opposition to what is regarded as a foreign religion. Possibly now that the connection between Spain and these islands has been broken and the people have been brought under the dominion of the United States, they will learn that both civil and religious liberty have been assured them by a Protestant government. The determined opposition of the Moros, however, does not promise much for the betterment of conditions under which missionary work may be undertaken.

We shall not pursue the advance of Islam in Malaysia

[26] *Preaching of Islam*, pp. 325, 326.

by any account of the efforts of Moslem missionaries to introduce the religion of the Quran into New Guinea and the many smaller islands in the Archipelago. Our survey has brought before us a vast missionary work covering centuries of Moslem endeavour, which has brought under the sway of Islam not less than fifty millions of people in the farther East, in China and Malaysia. It is true that in these regions, the Moslems are for the most part ignorant, that their religion is largely an imposition of the Moslem creed upon the animism of the old faith, that those of Malaysia in particular are superstitious and addicted to almost all the evils that are prohibited by the Quran, eating of pork, drinking and gambling; but it is also true that thousands of pilgrims annually visit Mecca and return as Hajjis, full of bigotry and a fiery zeal for Islam. In 1874 the number of pilgrims from Java alone was 33,802 and in 1886 that number rose to 48,237. A writer in the Report of the Centenary Conference on Protestant Missions alluding to the influence of Moslem pilgrimage on Islam in the Malay Archipelago remarks that while the increase of facilities of communication with Arabia may account in some measure for the large increase in the number of pilgrims, "this by no means diminishes the importance of the fact, especially as the Hajjis, whose numbers have grown so rapidly, have by no means lost in quality what they gained in quantity; on the contrary there are now amongst them many more thoroughly acquainted with the doctrines of Islam, and wholly imbued with Moslem fanaticism and hatred against the unbelievers, than there formerly were." [27]

[27] *Report Centenary Conference*, vol. i, p. 21.

The influence of a Protestant government amid such a people as the Malay Mohammedans is at once the hope and menace of missions in Malaysia. As far back as 1885 the number of schools for Mohammedans was 16,760, in which were taught 255,148 students. These schools are open to all classes and inasmuch as the language of the Mohammedans has been adopted as the official language of the Dutch Government, except in Java, this language becomes the medium of communication between the rulers and the ruled. The consequence is that every man who would hold office must learn the language of the Moslems. This brings the most intelligent men of every tribe under the influence of Moslem teachers and so must tend to further the Moslem propaganda. The hope is that general enlightenment of the Moslem himself will work out his intellectual salvation and enable him to see the fundamental weakness of the claim of the Quran to be the Word of God.

Here then is a new field for missions. Little or nothing has been done for the twenty million Hoi-Hois of China. Scarcely more has been done in Malaysia. A few have gathered up the crumbs from the table spread for heathen neighbours. No one so far as we know has had these fifty millions of the Far East laid upon his heart and gone forth to tell them of Him who is the only sinless prophet of Islam, to tell of Him who lives in glory, the heaven-appointed intercessor for sinners, to tell of Him who has atoned for sin, to tell of Him who he believes shall come again to earth to deliver the faithful from the hand of the great Antichrist. Is it not high time that the Christian Church should awake from its sleep of indifference towards the Moslem world? Too often, under the leadership of men filled with mistaken zeal of a Peter the Hermit, Christians have sought to convert the Moslem by the sword. Too often has she looked in vain for the legislator to aid her. Now comes the call of the Master Himself, especially in behalf of the ninety millions of the followers of Islam dwelling under the flags of Holland and England. Who will hear it? Who will obey?

I

PRESENT CONDITION OF MOSLEMS IN INDIA AND THE FAR EAST

THE Great Mogul no longer rules in India. After the rebellion of 1857 the control of the country passed out of the hands of the East India Company and India was placed under the immediate control of the English Government. With this change came the confirmation in authority of a number of Indian Chiefs, Hindu and Mohammedan, who have since ruled over their principalities in varied degrees of independence, some as Rajas and Maharajas, some as Nawabs and Nizams, others as noblemen of lesser degree. All are under the rule of the one great Indian Empire with the viceroy in supreme control. The principal Mohammedan rulers are the Nizam of Hyderabad, who rules over a state covering eighty-one thousand eight hundred and seven square miles with a population of about eleven million; the Begum of Bhopal, whose dominions comprise six thousand eight hundred and seventy-four square miles with a population of one million, the Nawabs of Bhawulpur, Maler Kotla, Loharu and others with lesser dominion.

Of the sixty-two millions of Moslems in India, less than seven millions are under native rulers of their own religious faith. Now, when we consider that for many centuries they had been in control and had practically directed the affairs of state in the great political centres in India, we should naturally have expected them to have secured a leading position under the regime inaugurated by the British conquest. It will be profitable to recount some of the reasons why this was not so.

The first influence operating against Moslem advancement at this period, and we may say every period of their history, has been the unprogressive character of the religion of Islam. Everything with the Mohammedan is as it were cast in a mould. This mould was made in eternity and determines the form of all things in time in accord with the divine decree, so that the idea of possible improvement or development beyond what is revealed is in the nature of the case impious. Everything necessary to Moslem perfection is to be found in the Quran, the Traditions and the deliverances of the Mujtahids.

The practical effect of this fatalistic teaching is to bring down the individual and national life to the very narrow limits of the teaching of the mullahs, or to the round of duties required by custom. The progressive movements, recorded by historians in the reigns of the Caliphs of Bagdad and Cordova, or of the Sultans of the Mogul Empire, were made not because of, but in spite of the teachings of orthodox Islam. Accordingly what was accomplished in the artistic and literary age which covered the reigns of Akbar the Great, Jahangir and Shah Jehan was due to influences foreign to Islam; and what was done was in a great measure undone by the fierce repressive measures adopted by the Moslem zealot, Aurangzeb, who undertook to bring the Empire back to the norm of Islam. At the close of his reign the Empire fell to pieces and the disunited fragments were unable to endure the onslaught of the Marathas in the south and west and of the Sikhs in the north. A long period of internecine warfare and anarchy resulted in the breaking up of the social and intellectual fabric of the Moslems in India. Education was limited to the schools at a very few centres and the teaching of the mullahs in the local mosques. The range of the instruction given was limited to the reading and writing of the Arabic character, along with a knowledge of Persian necessary for the performance of the duties of the public offices. In the higher schools at Delhi, Agra and Lucknow the education given was limited to the seven sciences of language, logic, rhetoric, jurisprudence, theology, exegesis and mathematics. Most of these had special relation to the knowledge of and the propagation of the religion of Islam. Secular knowledge, especially of physical science, has always been regarded by orthodox Moslems as dangerous to the faith and for this reason has been discouraged. Moreover, in the disturbed condition of the country during the two centuries preceding the establishment of British rule, the amount of education given, even along the narrow lines already described, was naturally very small. At the same time the ignorance of the vast majority of the mullahs led to extreme narrowness of thought and intense bigotry among the people. Under conditions like these, operating so persistently against the progress of Indian Moslems in social and intellectual life, we are prepared to understand how it was that when the way was opened up by the missionaries to give the people of India the advantages of western science and knowledge, the Mohammedan mullahs everywhere discouraged the people from sending their children to the mission schools. Only a few of the poorer people were willing to allow their boys to attend them, and that, too, when a monthly stipend was given to each pupil.

When later on the Government undertook to establish a system of public instruction and pledged the people that there would be no religious instruction given, many Moslems who had been unwilling to send their boys to the Christian schools were willing to patronise the secular schools of the Government. They desired that their boys should acquire the knowledge which would fit them for service in the Government offices. Nevertheless those who thus patronised the secular schools of Government formed a very small minority even in the cities, while in the country, the mass preferred to bring up their sons in the agricultural calling of their fathers, or else induce them to take service in the army or in the police corps. And so it came about that the schools were for the most part patronised by the Hindu and Christian population rather than by the Moslems. The consequence was that the numerous offices, open to those who had acquired the English education necessary to fit for duty, were closed to the Moslems, who had refused to qualify their young men for them. Hindus and Christians took the lead.

To amend this state of things and at the same time avoid the secularising influences of the Government schools, the Moslems organised numerous schools under the direction of the *Anjuman-i-Himayat-i-Islam,* the "Society for the Aid of Islam." These schools undertook to impart a knowledge of the English language and of western science as taught in the Indian Government schools. They sought at the same time to instil into the minds of the students a knowledge of the Arabic language and the tenets of Islam. These schools met with the approval of the Government and the sympathy of the Christian public, and yet they have rarely exhibited the efficiency of the rival schools. On the whole, however, they have done much to advance the social and intellectual condition of the Mussulmans. They have aroused a more progressive spirit among the people; and while their value to orthodox Islam may be questioned, they have raised up a class of men who have secured some of the emoluments of public office and the influence which official position and wealth usually bring with them.

Perhaps the institution which has done most to further the social and material interests of Mohammedans in India is the college at Aligarh, founded by the late Sir Sayyad Ahmad Khan, who was most liberally aided by Sir William Muir, then Lieutenant Governor of the Northwest Provinces. For some time this college was discredited by the orthodox leaders, because of the rationalistic teachings of Sir Sayyad Ahmad Khan, but the more liberal spirit bred through English education in the mission and government schools has rapidly grown, so that to-day all educated Moslems are proud of their great college, which may yet become the Moslem University of India. It should not be forgotten that this important advance in the intellectual and material interest of Indian Moslems has been largely promoted by the mission schools and colleges in India. The Presbyterian Churches of Scotland and America have established a system of schools graded up from the primary school to the middle or grammar school and from the middle to the high school and finally from the high school to the college in every one of which many Moslem youth have been receiving an education. Colleges are carried on by these missions in all the great cities, Calcutta, Madras, Bombay, Nagpur, Indore, Hazarabagh, Allahabad, Lahore and Rawal Pindi. Other missionaries are carrying on similar colleges in Amritsar, Peshawur, Delhi, Agra, and other cities, in all of which Moslems have been educated. The sons of weavers and tailors and cooks, who were among the first students of the mission schools, were thereby enabled to secure lucrative positions in the public service or to become masters in the mission and government schools. Their success naturally inspired others to seek for education in the mission schools. Many Mohammedan parents prefer to patronise the mission schools rather than the Islamia schools because of the superior training received in mission institutions, thus insuring a surer entry into government service.

And yet with all the advantages arising out of the awakened interest of Moslems for western education, the community is still far behind in the race for the highest places open to all classes of Indian young men.

There is, however, a sphere in the political life

of the country in which the Moslem is much to the fore. In all the subordinate offices of the revenue and judicial departments, in public works, in the police department and in the army, where especially the Urdu or Persian languages are used, the Moslem is found. In these places the Moslem who is anxious to win over his unbelieving countrymen has an opportunity to exert a great influence. This is especially true of the rural communities, where a teacher or a police inspector, a collector of revenue or a contractor on the railroad, occupies a position of authority and wisdom, which greatly increases his influence. He is able to speak the village dialect or language, and is thereby always able to get nearer to the people than his English superior in office. In a real sense it may be said of the Moslem that he speaks every language in India and is therefore able to influence the people widely.

The question has more than once been raised as to whether a Moslem can consistently be a loyal subject to a Christian king. The Moslem in India has no hesitation in saying yes in reply to this question. His reason is that inasmuch as the English Government gives him absolute liberty in the profession of his faith and in the propagation of the same; and further, since he possesses the same political rights as others resident in the land, therefore India may be regarded as a *Dar-ul-Islam* or Land of Islam.[1] Just what he would say were he persuaded that he no longer needed the sup-

[1] The question as to whether India is to be regarded as *Dar-ul-Harb* or *Dar-ul-Islam* is well discussed by Dr. W. W. Hunter in his book *Indian Musalmans.* See Hughes, *Dictionary of Islam*, pp. 69, 70.

port of the present beneficent rule of the Christian, we need not conjecture. At the present time the Mohammedans of India pledge their loyalty to the Government and whilst their present position is no doubt humiliating to those who look back with pride to the Moslem Empire of the great Mogul, whose splendid monuments still testify to their grandeur and glory, they seem as a whole to accept the situation as being the will of Allah and faithfully carry out the behests of the powers that be.

The fact is that the Indian Moslems never have been able to maintain their hold on the Indian Empire except by constantly drawing upon the resources of the Moslem nations in the west. The Hindus were rapidly gaining the upper hand long before the English came in as a conquering force. The Delhi Kings were mere puppets in the hands of Maratha princes. The Sikhs had overthrown the Moslem dominion in the Punjab. To such a low degree were they reduced that the mullahs were forbidden to cry the Azan, to call the faithful to prayer! The strong hand of the Sikh chieftains, like that of the Rajputs of the olden time, repelled every attempt of the Afghan to raid upon the rich plains of Hindustan. The coming of the English was the coming of a delivering host, which once more made it possible for Islam to recover her place as a great religious power in India. Her political interests are bound up in the perpetuity of Christian dominion, and her hope of advancement beyond her Hindu rival is dependent upon her intellectual and moral progress.

Let us now turn to notice rather briefly the moral

condition of the Moslems in India. As we have already seen, India was subject for centuries to the predatory raids of the conquering hordes of Moslems from the west. Like swarms of locusts, myriads of Arabs, Persians, Turks, Afghans, Mongols and Tartars poured into India. Many came to plunder the treasure hoards of the Hindus and returned to enjoy the spoils of war; but each invasion left behind some who were fascinated by the warm rich plains in the lands they had conquered and who chose to remain. They married the women of the land and became the progenitors of a class or caste, and so it came to pass that among the Moslems of India we have many classes claiming descent from noble families in Arabia, Persia, Turkey and elsewhere.

Then again, there were whole tribes of the people, Hindus, and aborigines, who were converted, retaining most of their tribal customs and manners. Hence we have whole towns and villages of Rajput Mussulmans, large communities of Musallies, who belong to the Sweeper class, and other communities known as Jats, Biloch, Moguls, etc. Scores of castes are held in common by Hindus, Sikhs and Mohammedans.

These facts will sufficiently emphasise the complexity of Moslem society and the almost kaleidoscopic character of their family life and social customs. While there is nothing in the religion of Islam to prevent promiscuous intermarriage between the various classes, yet in many cases such intermarriage is unusual. Racial and family pride, especially in the case of high caste Hindu converts, perhaps accounts for such class exclusiveness. Then caste has its advantages as well as its disadvantages, and serves to bind the various sections of society together into guilds or brotherhoods, which enable them to coerce both the refractory members within and the enemies of their order without. This recognition of caste too has no doubt been of much advantage to the Moslems in their dealings with their Hindu neighbours. It is a defence against aggression and a safeguard against social disintegration. Because of this recognition of caste the Moslem and the Hindu may draw water from the same well and in various ways have an intercourse with one another that is quite impossible to the Christian.

We have here an example of the adaptability of Islam to the peculiar customs of various nations and races. Among the tribes of Central Asia the women retain their freedom as in the olden time. So it was among the Moors of Spain. This too, notwithstanding the command of the Prophet. Islam knows no caste, except the one brotherhood of religion, and yet in India the Moslem is more or less caste-ridden.

These conditions have much to do with the low moral standards among Indian Moslems generally. The position of womanhood is never high in Moslem lands. In India, where centuries of ruthless warfare numbered womanhood among the lawful spoils of war and where female slaves were sold in the markets like cattle, and this too with the sanction of the Moslem religion, it is not wonderful that the general status of women is low. Illiteracy among them is well nigh universal. The census of 1902 reports only 91,059 women out of a total Moslem population of 62,458,077 as being able to read and write.

The polygamy practised so commonly by the well to do or wealthy classes works out in the direction not only of degrading womanhood, but also leads to the moral degradation of the family life. The boast of Moslems is that their system of plural marriages guards them against the pest houses so commonly found in Christian lands. But any one acquainted with the social life of Mohammedans knows how fallacious such statements really are. The vast number of men who have multiplied wives by the permission to divorce them for almost any reason, and often without reason, are only offset by the vast number of men who continually practise the many nameless vices of the East, vices which are almost unknown among the Western nations. These have exercised and still continue to work out a most disastrous influence upon the physical and mental life of the Indian Mohammedans. Purity among young men and purity in the home are wanting. The effect upon the race is manifest to all careful observers. A very significant fact is the absence of information upon this very delicate subject in almost all books written upon the Mussulmans of India, or for that matter on Moslems anywhere.

If we turn to the question of veracity and general probity, we fail to find any greater degree of truthfulness and honesty among them than there is among the Hindus generally. They do not trust one another. The inauguration of joint-stock companies, even in these modern times, is most difficult because of the general distrust of the people one for another. On this subject the late Dr. John Murdoch wrote as follows:

"Religion has become divorced from morality. It is a mere outward thing, a round of unmeaning rites and ceremonies, of prayers in an unknown tongue, of pilgrimages to the shrines of dead men, a means of hindering progress, of degrading and not of elevating humanity, of separating man from and not binding him to the God of holiness, of justice and love." [2]

The Superintendent of the Census of the Punjab and Northwest Frontier Province for 1902 notes some of the characteristics of the Moslems in these provinces in these words: "It is hardly possible to take up a Punjab Settlement Report without finding a lament over the shortcomings of the Mohammedan as a cultivator; his lack of energy, his thriftlessness, his capacity for getting hopelessly into debt: and in the towns, no part of the population felt the effects of scarcity more than the Mohammedan artisan classes of Delhi, Amritsar and Lahore." [3]

Major Drurie Osborn, in his *Islam under the Arabs*, p. 93, makes the following remarks which are equally true of Islam under the Moguls: "There is to be found in Mohammedan history all the elements of greatness—faith, courage, endurance, self-sacrifice; but, closed within the narrow walls of a rude theology and barbarous polity, from which the capacity to grow and the liberty to modify have been sternly cut off, they work no deliverance upon the earth. They are strong only

[2] *Religion of the World*, p. 166.
[3] *Census of India*, 1901, vol. xvii, p. 114.

for destruction. When that work is over, they either prey upon each other, or beat themselves to death against the bars of their prison house. No permanent dwelling place can be erected on a foundation of sand; and no durable or humanising polity upon a foundation of fatalism, despotism, polygamy and slavery. When Mohammedan states cease to be racked by revolutions, they succumb to the poison diffused by a corrupt moral atmosphere."

What is thus true in a general way as related to the political history of Moslem countries, is also true of the people in their social or communal life. Allusion has been made to the poverty and general thriftlessness of the Moslem farmer resulting in his being hopelessly in debt to the Hindu money lender. One has only to tour through the country anywhere in India to be convinced of the truth in this matter. The Hindu or Sikh villages will usually present the appearance of comfort and cleanliness, if not of wealth, while the evidences of neglect and careless management, of poverty and squalor will confront him in every Moslem town. This too is only equalled by the ignorance of the people. "Do not trouble to talk to us, sir, we are ignorant: We are like dumb beasts," is the greeting offered to the missionary, who would present to them the claims of the Christian religion. "We know nothing but this, that God is One and Mohammed is the Prophet of God." When one considers that most of these cultivators of the soil are the children of converts to Islam, he is reminded of Major Osborn's words, "It [Islam] reproduces in its new converts the characteristics of its first—their impenetrable self-esteem, their unintelligent scorn, and blind hatred of all other creeds. And thus the capacity for all further advance is destroyed; the mind is obdurately shut to the entrance of any purer light."[4]

This senseless stupidity and absence of any rational energy has recently received a new illustration in the stolid opposition of the Mohammedan population to the endeavour of the Indian Government to stay the advance of the bubonic plague by a rigid system of quarantine and segregation. In many cities where plague had broken out, the Government placed skilled physicians to aid and advise the people in every way known to modern science how to protect themselves from this awful scourge. They were advised on the appearance of the plague to leave their houses at once and camp in the fields outside the stricken village. If the disease should invade the home, the sick should be separated from the well and be placed in a tent or hut outside, or better still be taken to the plague hospital for treatment. When any one died, the people were advised not to unnecessarily expose themselves to contagion at the funeral. But all this good advice was lost upon the Moslems. They disobeyed every order and rejected all advice. They stayed in their infected homes and villages. They visited their sick friends, often accompanied by their children. They went in troops to the burial grounds, taking turns as often as possible to aid in carrying the bier to the graveyard. They returned to their homes and slept in them as

[4] Quoted by Dr. John Murdoch in *The Religions of the World*, p. 166.

usual. No wonder they died off like flies. The mullahs applauded and even pronounced a curse upon any one who refused to thus expose himself to this dread disease. Does not God reign? Has he not written the decree? Can any one die before his time comes? Will any one be so impious as to try to prevent the fulfilment of God's purpose? While thus the mullah will argue, he does not stop to inquire why he essays the practice of medicine, nor does any one seem to think it strange that he is asked to pay the mullah for medical advice..

Among the artisan classes one notices the same want of energy, almost every one being satisfied to eke out a miserable subsistence by rendering a daily tale of service to his employer. The master may be a Hindu banker and merchant, who holds a mortgage upon his service for years to come; or he may be a Mohammedan merchant-manufacturer, who supplies the materials while the artisan works out the manufactured product for a wage that will barely keep body and soul together. In these Indian sweat shops, the great mass of the Moslem artisans are employed. The contractor so far as possible sublets his contract. The small contractor employs his workmen. The head or master workman permits the ordinary artisan to help on condition that he gives him a percentage of the wages, and so the grinding process goes on, and the wage-earner plods on under a social and economic system scarcely better than that of slavery. Of the labouring classes in general it is pathetic to hear them say that they only ask a pound of flour (*Ser atta*) as the reward for a day's labour, or to learn from the lips of an educated land-owner, as the writer has done, that the average monthly pay of a farm labourer is not more than $1.75. Ordinarily skilled workmen, carpenters, masons, painters and glaziers receive no more than twelve to twenty-five cents a day, which is more than twice the pay received thirty years ago.

One of the blessings incident upon the terrible inroads of the plague, which has been especially fatal among the young men belonging to the artisan and agricultural classes, is the rise of wages owing to the great scarcity of labourers in the labour market.

In the cities the various classes of workmen are adopting the methods of the labour unions to some extent and striking for higher wages, but so long as the labourer is debtor to his employer, little relief can be secured by a strike. The employer can afford to lock out the labourer, but the labourer cannot afford to quit work, which means to starve.

Under such conditions it is impossible to expect any great energy or enterprise to appear among the mass of these poor wage-earners, who must live from hand to mouth. On the other hand the wealthier classes of the Moslem community easily fall victims to the allurements of vice, instead of using their wealth and opportunity to build up industrial and mercantile institutions which would benefit their country and countrymen. There are some men who are active in such laudable enterprises—men who are worthy of those Hindu and Arab traders who once ruled the Eastern Seas, and whose herds of camels bore the products of the East to the West as some of them still do. Many, however, fail to do anything beyond maintaining an expensive establishment, wasting their means in riotous living. Strange as it may appear, many of the most notorious users of intoxicants are Moslems. Brandy and whisky as well as opium and hasheesh account for the failure of many otherwise promising lives.

It may not be out of place to make special mention of this matter of drunkenness among Moslems in India and elsewhere. The opinion is held by many good people in Christian lands that the Moslems are a sort of modern Rechabites whose example may be held up as a model for Christian imitation and the whole Mohammedan community is regarded as strictly abstinent from all intoxicating liquors. Such indeed they should be; for the command of the Arabian prophet is to the following effect: "Satan seeketh to sow dissension and hatred among you by means of wine and lots, and to divert you from remembering God and from prayers. Will ye not therefore abstain from them?" (Chap. v. 93). But Moslems have not been much more consistent in this matter than their Christian neighbours. The old adage to "drink like a Turk" has had frequent illustrations among Moslems in India. Several of the most noted of the governors and kings of Delhi were notorious winebibbers. The following story, quoted by Stanley Lane Poole, from a Moslem chronicler, Baihaki,[5] tells how Mas'ud, the son of the great Mahmud of Ghazni, used to see his fellow-topers "under the tables." "The serious business of the day began: 'Let us to it without ceremony,' cried the Amir: 'we are come into the country, and we will drink.' Fifty goblets and flagons

[5] *Mediaeval India*, p. 37.

of wine were brought from the pavilion into the garden, and the cups began to go round. 'Fair measure,' said the Amir, 'and equal cups—let us drink fair!' They grew merry and the minstrels sang. One of the courtiers had finished five tankards—each held nearly a pint of wine—but the sixth confused him, the seventh bereft him of his senses and at the eighth he was consigned to his servants. The doctor was carried off at his fifth cup; Khalil Dawud managed ten; Sayabiruz nine, and then they were taken home; everybody rolled or was rolled away, till only the Sultan and the Khwaja Abd-ar-Razzak remained. The Khwaja finished eighteen goblets and then rose saying, 'If your slave has any more he will lose both his wits and his respect for your Majesty.' Mas'ud went on alone, and after he had drunk twenty-seven full cups, he too arose, called for water and prayer-carpet, washed, and recited the belated noon and sunset prayers together as soberly as if he had not tasted a drop; then mounted his elephant and rode to the palace. 'I witnessed the whole of this scene with mine own eyes, I, Abu-l-Fazl,' says Baihaki."

Such orgies were characteristic of the Turkish rulers of Ghazni. Of the Emperor Jahangir, Sir Thomas Roe writes and among other habits of the great Mogul narrates the following: "He then says his prayers and has a meal of four or five sorts of well-dressed meats, of which he eateth a bit to stay his stomach, drinking once of his strong drinke. Then cometh forth into a private roome, where none can come but such as himself nominateth (for two years I was one of his attendants here). In this place he drinketh other five cupfuls, which is the portion that the physicians alot him. This done he eateth opium, and then being in the height of his drinke, he layeth himself down to sleep."[6]

The influence of these royal drunkards was no doubt most baneful during their lifetime and their example has been followed by many during all the years gone by.

This statement is important because even so learned a man as the writer of the article on Mohammedanism in the International Encyclopedia asserts that excepting a few who have come under European influences, the Moslems never use intoxicating liquors. That Europeans have shown, and do still show, a shocking example of intemperance before Moslem peoples is true, but it may be questioned whether the intemperance of the Mussulmans has not been a stumbling block to many Europeans. It is quite certain that Sir Thomas Roe, who sat in the private room of the Emperor Jahangir for two years, would have had some difficulty in finding a larger and more constant consumer of intoxicants.

In China and Malaysia, the intellectual and moral condition of the Mohammedan population differs little from that of their neighbours. In China the Moslems, having adopted or maintained the customs of the Chinese, and for the most part concealing their religious character, are admitted to the competitive examinations and made eligible to office.

In Malaysia, the Netherlands Government carries on a system of public schools which educates the people in the language used by the Moslem population. This opens the way to the Moslem to secure the lucrative

6 Stanley Lane Poole's *Mediaeval India*, p. 305.

offices of government, whilst among the warlike and practically independent Acheenese the people enjoy the liberty and prosperity possible to a native government in a fairly prosperous country. As to the moral status of the people, it is that of Moslems generally. Slavery has been prohibited by the Dutch Government. Polygamy exists as in all Moslem lands. In general the conversion of the people to Islam does not seem to have done much to raise their moral ideals. In Borneo and the Philippine Islands the converts were taught to abstain from head hunting, the eating of swine's flesh, and the use of intoxicants. In all other respects they seem to be as treacherous and murderous as their heathen fellow countrymen. In general it may be said of India and the Far East, that while customs and manners have been changed and among the more uncivilised tribes vast improvement has been made, yet the moral standards of the Moslem are generally low. Slavery and polygamy are recognised by the sacred books, almost unlimited divorce is provided for by the laws of Islam; lying and deception are condoned, and a proud, domineering spirit is encouraged. Dr. John Murdoch in his book *The Religions of the World*, pp. 165, 166, says: "After twelve centuries of Islam, the Arabs are still what Mohammed found them, a nation of robbers." "All Moslem governments are despotisms." "Countries once rich and prosperous, renowned for their learning under Moslem rule, are now blighted and ruined, their people downtrodden and heartbroken; their fertility almost forgotten. Tyranny and intolerance, ignorance and sloth, crime and superstition hang like a curse over all things and blast even the very face of nature itself." Wherever the Moslems of India, China and the Far East enjoy something better than this normal condition of Moslem lands, they are indebted to the Christian and Confucian regime under which they live.

Looking at the Moslems in India and the regions eastward from the standpoint of religion, we find here all the various sects and schools which characterise Islam in the world. Of the four great schools of interpretation, Hanafiya, Malakiya, Shafii and Hanbali, the vast majority are Hanafiyahs, who stand for the Quran as the prime authority on all matters of faith and practice. This fact is of interest and encouragement to the missionary to Moslems. It gives him a strong fulcrum wherewith to move the hearts of men who believe in a divine revelation, and are open to the influence of the Scriptures which are attested by the Quran itself: "O, children of Israel, remember my favour wherewith I have favoured you, and believe in the revelation which I have sent down, confirming that which is with you" (Chap. ii. 39, 40). "We also caused Jesus, the Son of Mary, to follow the footsteps of the prophets, confirming him; and we gave him the Gospel, containing direction and light; confirming also the light which was given before it, and a direction and admonition unto those who fear God: that they who have received the Gospel might judge according to what God hath revealed therein" (Chap. v. 50, 51).

This attitude of the vast majority of Indian Moslems toward the thought of a divinely revealed religion, has a most important influence upon the spiritual life of the people. It makes the truth of God, so far as it has been conserved among the Moslem nations in the teaching of the Quran, effectual in the practical life of the people. There is always a strong influence exerted in favour of a pure monotheism as over against the idolatry of the heathen around them and even the idolatry found among the ignorant proselytes recently brought in from among the idolaters. And under the influences exerted by Protestant Christianity, we find among the more intelligent and consistent Moslems of to-day many who endeavour to get out of the Quran the best that is in it, and even to adapt many obscure passages to the higher teaching of the Gospel. The same influence is raising in many minds the question of reform in respect to the education and position of women. At a recent Congress of Indian Moslems, a leading Moslem in a most scholarly address urged upon his co-religionists the duty of educating their women in order that their children might have the benefit of the teaching of intelligent motherhood in the home. He went even further and plead for the abolition of the veil as necessary to the higher culture of Moslem womanhood. The influence of higher education among Mohammedans in general is to raise higher the ideals of religious life among them.

Among the heretical sects of Islam, the Shiahs, Sufis, Ahmadayyahs, and the votaries of the New Islam, there is often a decidedly near approach to Christian ideals. Many seem to be groping after a closer walk and communion with God, but they despair of reaching Him, who must to the student of the Quran ever remain "sterile in His inaccessible height." He ever "lets them feel that they can never be more than slaves, that nearness to Him is impossible." [7] The Sufi has striven to solve this difficulty by reviving the gnostic doctrine of the aeons, whereby he receives the thought of God revealing Himself by a process of self-limitation. The hope is that through the great historical facts of the Gospel, now so widely disseminated, these yearners after God may come to see Him incarnate in the Christ.

While it is true that there are many signs of a new religious life among the more enlightened Mohammedans of India, there are many more who, like the Hajjis of Malaysia, are being established in the narrowness of Arabian, and especially of Meccan theological teaching. This is probably due to pan-Islamic influences emanating from Constantinople. These are doing much, not only in India but also in Malaysia, to improve the condition of the great mass of Moslems, who are steeped in the corruption of idolatry and heathen usages. With these, religion is a custom and a tradition, which makes them more difficult to evangelise than their more enlightened co-religionists. "Ignorance and superstition have always been the worst foes of truth."

In China, the mass of the Moslems are ignorant of the sacred writings. Dr. Sell describes their religious condition in the following words: "The Chinese Moslems prohibit the use of tobacco, but opium smokers are numerous amongst them. Gambling and games are

[7] *Essays on Islam*, by Rev. E. Sell, D.D., M.R.A.S., p. 44.

illegal, but they evade this by saying that the Prophet only forbade games of hazard, and allowed draughts and chess which depend on the skill of the player. As a matter of fact, dice, cards, and betting at cock-fights are common, and the Moslems equally with other Chinese are gamblers. Usury is prohibited. Musical instruments must not be used in private or in public. Vocal music also is improper, though passages from the Quran may be chanted at the time of prayer. Dancing is altogether wrong. It is also forbidden to make statues of men or figures of animals, but photographs (being made by the sunlight) are allowed. Astrology, divinations, magic, and all calculations based on auguries and dreams, are utterly condemned. In this respect the Moslems have not fallen under the spell of the Chinese custom and practice in these matters. Among themselves they use the ordinary Moslem salutations, but to outsiders they use the form common to all. . . . Moslems in China possess much religious liberty, but they purchase this by conforming to pagan practices and ceremonial, and by a subserviency to the prejudices of the state officials and of the literary classes in a manner unusual amongst their co-religionists in other lands." [8]

In general it may be remarked that among all Moslems there is an absence of the sense of personal guilt before God on account of sin. The Moslem is satisfied with a perfunctory observance of the ritual. He has little regard for the sins of the carnal nature as catalogued by St. Paul, Gal. v. 19-21, excepting those of idolatry and witchcraft, and even these, as we have al-

[8] Sell's *Essays on Islam*, pp. 215, 216.

ready noted, are continually committed by the multitudes who pray and make offerings to the saints and tombs of dead dervishes, who believe in charms and talismans.

Their faith in the merit of prayers and the repetition of the *Kalima,* "God is One and Mohammed is the Prophet of God," makes them believe that God will not take any account of their sin and that if He should, they will enter Paradise through the merit of their profession and the intercession of the Prophet.

In regard to Christians and the Christian faith, the teaching of the mullahs places Moslems upon their guard whenever approached by the evangelist. Even the Bible and Christian books are tabooed, so that their eyes are blinded and their ears are shut against the Gospel.

There are, however, multitudes who have lost faith in orthodox Islam, and who may be seeking after some way of hope for the life to come, or who are quite indifferent to all religion. Many, as we have seen, belong to heretical sects, who refuse to believe in all the teachings of the Moslem doctors, and yet who have faith in Islam because they believe in the Prophet, though they cannot understand his book. There are others, and these in an increasingly large number, who have had access to the Gospel and who are seeking to know the truth of its claims. Most of these are men educated in mission schools or who have been influenced by the Christian literature which is being sown broadcast throughout India. Some of these turn aside and join the ranks of the reformers—the Ahmaddiyahs or the followers of the New Islam, of which we shall have occasion to speak in another place.

The impact of Protestant Christian Missions has been keenly felt in India, and in the Dutch East Indies. The result has been the arousing of the Moslem leaders. Societies have been formed, schools of theology have been established, and many preachers have been trained to meet the Christian propaganda. Presses have been set up and books and periodicals in both the English and vernacular languages have been published. Tracts and booklets are scattered abroad filled with the objections and misrepresentations of Gospel teaching so common among European unbelievers and even atheists. Every social influence is brought to bear against the men or women who would give ear to Christian teaching. Social ostracism and even violence is threatened when other means fail to deter. The conflict is here and must continue until the truth prevails. It is for you and me to consider well our part. It is for us to set our feet solidly upon the infallible truth of God's word and in the spirit of love and purity, to patiently and persistently hold up before these Moslems the person and teachings of the Lord Jesus, who is to every true Mohammedan a holy prophet,—who is also a prophet ascended and glorified in heaven,—who is destined to return to the earth again to restore the true faith of God among men. He is the hope of Israel, and He is also the hope of Ishmael.

V

MISSIONS TO MOSLEMS IN INDIA AND THE FAR EAST

EARLY in the Christian Era the Gospel of Jesus was preached in India. Traditions, still alive among the Syrian Christians of Southern India, credit the founding of their churches to the Apostle Thomas. It is probable that the work was done by certain disciples of that Apostle.

How widely extended the influence of this Church in India ever became is now a mere matter of conjecture. It is probable that the work began along the coast and gradually extended back into the hills where the community entrenched itself and, amidst the turmoils which later on filled India with strife and bloodshed, maintained its existence.

By the time the Mohammedan armies began to make inroads upon India in the West and North, the Syrian Church had ceased to be a strong religious factor, if, indeed, it ever had been, in South India. Certain it is that we have no record of any effort on its part to influence in any way either the religious faith of the Mohammedans or of their Hindu neighbours. Accepting practically the social customs and even the manners and dress of the Hindus, they seem to have passed current as one of the religious cults of Hinduism.

Wherever the Moslem conqueror came within their territory, they secured peace by submitting to pay the usual poll tax. Indeed, Islam itself never secured a strong hold upon the Malabar country.

Whether Nestorian missionaries ever entered India proper, is doubtful. Their journeying eastward seems to have been through Persia into Tartary by way of the great trade routes between China and Western Asia. Of these routes we know little previous to the thirteenth century, but we may fairly conclude that these routes were known long before. Marco Polo, and the Chinese pilgrims Fah-hien and Huan-Chwang, in their Journals,[1] describe northern routes which have been clearly traced and identified with those highways of travel by which the hordes of Tartars and Mongols were later on able to enter Persia and Asia Minor to the west, and India and Egypt to the southwest. Marco Polo makes distinct mention of finding Christians of the Nestorian sect in Armenia, Georgia, Bagdad, Tabriz, Kashgar, Samarkand, Yarkand, Su-Chow, Kan-Chow, and other cities in Northern China. The number of Christians at that time was probably not very great, and yet he says that there were three large churches in the city of Kan-Chow.[2] He tells of a great battle fought between the armies of Kublai Khan and his relative Nayan, a grandson of the great Genghis-Khan, who had rebelled against the Grand Khan. This prince was said to have espoused the Christian faith and to have caused a great

[1] E. H. Parker in *China, Her History, Diplomacy and Commerce*, pp. 60-62.

[2] *Marco Polo's Travels*, Bohn's Library. See references in Index under *Christians*.

banner of the religion to be carried before his army. In that army were Jews, Moslems, and Christians. The battle was bloody. But the banner of the cross failed to save the rebel prince and his cause. The Grand Khan was victorious and the rebellious Nayan was put to death. The Jews and Mohammedans began to reproach the Christians, saying, "Behold the state to which your vaunted banners and those who follow them are reduced." These derisions led to a protest from the Christians, which was laid before the Grand Khan, who ordered the Jews and Moslems to be brought before him, and having sharply rebuked them, he said, "If the cross of Christ has not proved advantageous to the party of Nayan, the effect has been consistent with reason and justice, inasmuch as he was a rebel and a traitor to his lord, and to such wretches it could not afford its protection. Let none, therefore, presume to charge with injustice the God of the Christians, who is himself the perfection of goodness and justice."

Marco Polo goes on to say that this Tartar chief did honour to all religions in his dominion. When asked to give his reasons for so doing, he said: "There are four great prophets who are reverenced and worshipped by the different classes of mankind. The Christians regard Jesus Christ as their Divinity; the Saracens, Mahomet; the Jews, Moses; and the idolaters Sogomombas-Kan (Sakia Muni), the most eminent among their idols. I do honour and show respect to all these four and invoke to my aid whichever amongst them is in truth supreme in heaven."[3]

These stories indicate what they were no doubt in-

[3] Marco Polo's *Travels*, pp. 167, 168.

tended to illustrate: the very general influence which these four foreign religions had upon the great Khan of the Tartar race, and also upon many of his people. The single inference which concerns us just now is that Nestorian Christianity had found its way into the region we know as Chinese Tartary. It had no doubt found its way along the great highways of trade. So extensive was the spread of Nestorianism that its organised government, modified no doubt in accord with the tribal usage, gave rise to the story of a dynasty of Christian chiefs known as that of Prester John. Christianity was no doubt recognised by the very tolerant Tartar Khans as one of the religious cults of their dominion. This opinion receives confirmation from the discovery in the seventeenth century (1620), in the city of Si-ngan-fu (Hsi-ngan-fu), of a rock inscription dated 781 A. D., which told of the coming of a Syrian missionary, Clopeunn, into the Province of Shen-si in the year 635, and of the rapid spread of Christianity in that region.

There was then a Nestorian Christianity in China, when in the seventh century Moslem missionary traders and teachers found their way there, as we have already explained in a former chapter. How far it had lost its missionary character we cannot say. It no doubt suffered under the change of emperors and dynasties, and it may have been even tolerant of the ever-increasing and all-conquering religion of the Arab, and later on of the Turk. And when the power of the Mongols was finally given to Islam and the hordes of Tamerlane drew the sword to propagate the faith, the Nestorian Church probably met the fate of the Oriental Churches generally. As in Egypt, Syria and Persia, so in China, most of the Christians found it to their advantage to accept Islam.

So far then as the Nestorian Church is concerned, we have little or no reason to believe that it realised its duty to tell the Moslems of China the story of Jesus and his love. The most we can say is that for a long period, covering not less than six centuries, they maintained in some degree their churches and their forms of worship and, as in the case already noted, they showed a zeal for the honour of their faith.

On the other hand, while the weak and discouraged and ignorant Christians were slowly absorbed into the Moslem community, there does not seem to have been that violent animosity between Moslem and Christian that exists in other lands. A remarkable illustration of this fact was the immunity of the Christians in Yun-nan and Shen-si during the Panthay rebellion of 1856. When the Chinese Government planned a general slaughter of the Moslems, they rose up to retaliate and slew more than a million of Chinese, but spared the Christians. It is said these Dungan Moslems were the descendants of the Nestorian Christians who had accepted Islam.

The first serious effort to bring over the Tartar clans, who were rapidly turning from their crude heathenism to monotheism, was made by the Roman Catholic propaganda in the thirteenth century. While her purpose was to forestall Islam, her attention was directed especially to the Khans or rulers of the Tartar tribes. For a time their efforts had a show of success, a number of men in high places having avowed themselves to be followers of Christ. Some of the missionaries adopted Chinese dress and customs, even wearing the cue in order to win favour with the people. Some of them succeeded in getting into high offices under government and used their official influence to further the cause of Catholic missions among the Chinese. Nevertheless their efforts do not seem to have ever been directed toward the Christianising of the Moslems, but rather toward gathering into the Roman fold the Nestorian Christians and the conversion of the idolaters. They reported large accessions to their churches, but when later the fierce disputes between the Jesuits and the Dominican friars led to the active opposition of the Chinese Government and eventually to the suppression of the Catholic missions, most of the converts disappeared. Some were killed in the persecutions, others apostatised, while a few continued as secret believers. The Catholic Church had placed before it a grand opportunity. It was the possible chance of turning the Tartars under the dominion of the great Khans to the faith of the pure Gospel of Jesus Christ. They failed because they chose to follow the dictates of human wisdom rather than the guidance of the Holy Spirit. Two centuries later the opportunity to re-establish the Roman Catholic missions came, but nothing was done for the Moslems in China.

Toward the close of the sixteenth century the Society of the Jesuits, under the patronage of the King of Portugal, sent from Goa missionaries to North India. At that time the great Moslem Emperor Akbar had established his rule throughout India. He was tolerant of other faiths than that of Islam. The first of the Catholic Fathers was Hieronymo Xavier, who came bearing letters of introduction to the Great Mogul from the King of Portugal. Of the two great centres of mission work for the conversion of Indian Moslems, Agra and Lahore, Xavier chose the latter as his central station. He arrived in the year 1596 A. D., and spent about twelve years in that famous royal city of the Mogul Emperors, during which time he made a careful study of the Persian language and the tenets of Islam. He proclaimed himself a Christian priest who had renounced the pomp of this world in order to devote himself to the service of God and to teach Christians the way of salvation. His method of approach was that of a humble monk, anxious to discuss religious subjects in an unostentatious way. Many such discussions were held, the gist of which may be learned from a volume which he wrote, entitled *Aina i Haqq Numa,* "A Mirror Showing Truth," which has been preserved in the library of Queen's College in the University of Cambridge. This work has been translated by the Rev. S. Lee, A. M., Professor of Arabic in that University, accompanied by notes and comments. To this work I am indebted for much of what follows in regard to this mission to Indian Moslems.[4]

The great difficulty which constantly confronted this able missionary, and which still confronts all Roman Catholic missionaries in Moslem lands, was the neces-

[4] This work is entitled *Persian Controversies*, Cambridge, 1824, a work which might well be republished.

sity of defending image and saint worship. The difficulties confronting all Christian missionaries among Moslems, growing out of the doctrine of the Holy Trinity and the divinity and incarnation of the Son of God, are great. But these doctrines are among the mysteries of the faith and are based upon the plain teachings of the Scriptures of the Old and New Testaments, which maintain clearly the unity of the Godhead and continually denounce the sin of idolatry. Based upon this ground, the Moslem has no refuge from the charge of heresy and unbelief, because he denies the testimony of that Bible which the Quran claims to attest as the Word of God, unless he denies the genuineness and credibility of the Christian Books. But when it comes to the necessity of vindicating the Roman Catholic practice of praying to the Virgin Mary and the saints, the symbols of their faith, not to mention their reverence for relics and even the bones of saints, their cause becomes hopeless. I once asked a Catholic missionary how he approached the people in his teaching. Said I, "What do you first of all try to impress upon their minds?" He replied, "We tell them of the one true God and the sin of idolatry." "Well, then, how do you reconcile that teaching with the Church's teaching as to the Blessed Virgin and the intercession of saints?" Said he, "We do not tell them about those things at first!" It is easy to understand what the effect of such teaching would be in the case of a Mohammedan inquirer.

The teaching of the Jesuit missionary Hieronymo Xavier on the subject of the fundamental doctrines of

God, the Trinity, the Eternal Sonship and Incarnation of the Second Person of the Trinity, was clear and calculated to impress deeply the Moslem mind.

Of the Trinity, he said, "Although the essence is truly one, it consists (nevertheless), of three persons, the Father, the Son, and the Holy Ghost: one true God, without confusion of persons, or division of essence, or (such as) leaving the unity, should assume a plurality. This property of the Deity is infinite and such as can obtain in no other."

On the Sonship of Christ, after presenting the usual statement as to the necessity for incarnation in human nature and the purpose of the suffering, death and resurrection of Jesus, he goes on to tell why we should retain and reverence the images of Jesus and others, and also of the reverence due to the relics of the saints, because the approval of God is set upon such worship of the images and relics of the saints, by the wonderful miracles which are wrought upon those who reverence them! When this learned preacher gave a list of the Ten Commandments, he omitted the Commandment against image worship.

The missions of the Roman Catholic Church in the Malaysian Archipelago were established along the line of Portuguese and Spanish conquest. Like the wars carried on against the Mexicans, Peruvians and other heathen peoples in South America, the wars in the Indian Archipelago were waged largely in the interest of religion. The Cross was planted upon every island where the Catholic dominion was established. The sword and political influence were used with a zeal and fanaticism well-nigh as great as that of the Arab conquerors who preceded them.

This antagonism of the Mohammedan chiefs and traders, who had gained the supreme control in Malaysia, rendered futile all attempts to convert the people. The gospel of Spanish Christianity was a gospel of greed. No sincere attempt was made to win the people to the good news of Him who preached a gospel of peace. The Moslem was called upon to submit to the force of the conqueror. And for a time the work of converting the natives to Islam was impeded. The Portuguese added many names to the church rolls, but when Spain annexed Portugal, the missions were abandoned and the ignorant converts soon became Mohammedans, or lapsed into heathenism. The missions of the Church of Rome in the East received an almost fatal blow when the deceptions and frauds practised by some of the Jesuits were exposed. The Franciscan Fathers did good service in their endeavour to restore the cause. The missions still exist in India and China, but so far as the Moslem world is concerned, they have proved to be a failure. Their testimony has rather been against Christianity than for it. They have by their endeavour to uphold image worship aided the cause of Islam. This fact, even more than their political manœuvring, accounts for their failure to get even the respect of the Moslems in India and the Far East. Indeed, the Roman Catholic teachers have confirmed the Mohammedans in their errors and misconceptions of the truth as it is taught in the Christian Scriptures. History stands in evidence to prove that the mission to the great Mogul in India, with all its splendid opportunities of preaching before emperors and noblemen, failed to accomplish any practical result in the way of converting the Mohammedans to Christianity.

It remains for us to learn what Protestantism has accomplished in the work of Moslem evangelisation in India and the Far East.

The advent of the Dutch in the Indian Archipelago sealed the fate of the Spanish missions there. The only stronghold that remained to them was in the Philippine Islands, where they succeeded in converting the heathen, but failed to impose Christianity upon the Mohammedan population. The political scheme for the control of the Dutch East Indies included the segregation of the Islands against any missionary endeavour except that of the Holland Churches. Two missionaries of the American Board lost their lives in the attempt to establish a mission among a hill tribe in the Island of Sumatra.

The Dutch missions are carried on very systematically. For a time Moslems were angered by the refusal to allow them to visit Mecca. Long and bloody wars have been waged against the Acheenese in the Island of Sumatra. The Dutch are now in control, and with the establishment of schools for the native population, and the withdrawal of the prohibition against pilgrimage, there is a good prospect of permanent peace and quiet among all classes. The nominal adherents of Islam in those islands are very ignorant of their own religion. Much work has been done to bring them into the Church, and the success attending it has been most encouraging. The number of converts from Islam in Java and Sumatra is given in round numbers at eighteen thousand. Education in the national school system is given in the language of the Moslem population, so that the Christian community will not be left in ignorance, and many Moslem youth will be influenced in favour of Christianity by their contact with Protestant Christians in the schools and elsewhere. The Scriptures have been translated into the vernacular languages and a considerable literature has also been created. How well suited this is for the Moslem reader I have not been able to learn.

In the Philippine Islands there are now two hundred and fifty thousand Moslems, whose evangelisation is laid in a special manner upon the American Churches. Missions have been started in the Philippines by several Protestant societies, but as yet little has been done for the evangelisation of the Mohammedans. The American Board (Congregational) has opened a station on the island of Mindanao, almost entirely peopled by Mohammedan Moros, and as soon as possible they expect to extend the work among those people. The same is true of the twenty millions of Moslems in China, to whom, until very recently, no society has sent any missionaries. We are glad to hear that the China Inland Mission has felt called to undertake this duty. May God lead his servants and enable them to do an effective work!

The first deliberate effort of Protestant Christianity looking towards the evangelisation of Moslems in India began with the labours of the sainted Henry Martyn.

Entering upon his work in 1805, he began the study of the Urdu, Persian and Arabic languages, and soon began the work of translating the New Testament into Urdu and Persian. This was undertaken because it would make it possible for at least one-third of the Moslem world to read or hear read in their own language the holy *Injil* or New Testament.

The desire to completely revise the Persian translation of the New Testament led Henry Martyn to go to Persia, where his mission became a definite work for the conversion of Mohammedans. Here he was soon drawn into a long controversy with several of the most learned mullahs in Persia. The addresses on both sides of this debate were committed to writing, and form one of the most interesting and instructive presentations of the arguments, pro and con, for the defence and propagation of Christianity and Islam that can be found anywhere. This controversy has been translated and published in English by Professor Lee of Cambridge University.

The great work which Henry Martyn wrought was his translation of the Scriptures into the languages of the Moslems in India and Persia. Although this man of God had the privilege of baptising forty converts, only one was from Islam. That one was Mullah Sheikh Salih, who took the name Abdul Masih, and was afterwards ordained to the ministry by Bishop Heber. One other, and probably one among many, rose up in the city of Shiraz in Persia, to confess that his conversion was due to the teaching of Henry Martyn. This faithful missionary had once said, "Even if I never should see a native converted, God may design, by my patience and continuance in the work, to encourage future missionaries." Only the Judgment Day will reveal the extent of the influence of this man, who, with no Christain to tend or comfort him in his last illness, laid down his life at Tocat on the 16th of October, 1812. He was the forerunner of that noble band of missionaries of the Church Missionary Society, Bishop French, Hughes, Elmslie, Wade, Clark, Hooper, and others, who have emulated him in their endeavour to give the Gospel to the Moslems of India, Persia, Arabia, Afghanistan, Beluchistan, Egypt, and Central Africa.

From this time and onward, the missionaries of the English, American, European and Australian Protestant Churches undertook a definite work for the conversion of Moslems as well as of Hindus. The Scriptures in the Hindustani and Persian languages were published and scattered broadcast among the Mohammedan people able to read. Books and tracts specially suited to commend the Gospel and to answer the popular objections of Moslems were prepared and published and given away gratuitously to any one willing to read them.

Schools were established in which education was imparted through the medium of the languages spoken by Moslems, especially the Urdu or Hindustani, and the Persian languages. By and by English was also taught and the grade of the schools increased until the high school and the college were created. The increase of education served to widen the circle of influence. The Scriptures were translated into Bengali, Hindi, Punjabi,

Kashmiri, Sindhi, and Beluchi. To these were added the Scriptures in Arabic, which were translated and published at Beirut in Syria, and imported into India for use among the mullahs and maulvies. A suitable vernacular religious literature was also prepared for Moslem readers.

The missionary societies which have been specially active in this work are the Church Missionary Society, the Society for the Propagation of the Gospel, the London Missionary Society, the Churches of Scotland's Missions, the American Presbyterian Missions in North India, the United Presbyterian Mission, the American Methodist Episcopal Mission and the English and Australian Baptist Missions.

The methods of approach adopted by the missionaries in their preaching have not usually had special reference to Mohammedans, except in the extreme northwestern borders where the vast majority of the auditors are Mohammedans.

In the street and in the chapel the Moslems have been addressed along with Hindus and Sikhs, as men lying under condemnation before God because of sin; and Jesus Christ has been held up before them as the only Saviour of men. All have been earnestly invited to turn unto God by repentance and faith in Christ. As the languages used are usually understood by Moslems, and inasmuch as the Scriptures and books and tracts were printed in the character commonly used by Mohammedans, no one was more likely to feel himself specially addressed than the Moslem. No one would be more likely to appreciate the point of the preacher's remarks, and none more ready to oppose the missionary by raising objections to his teaching. Oftentimes the preaching almost imperceptibly changed its character and became a debate upon some point of doctrine, *e. g.*, the integrity of the Scriptures, the doctrine of the abrogation of the Scriptures, the inimitable style of the Quran, the sinfulness of the prophets, the miracles of Jesus, the absence of miracles and prophecy in the life of Mohammed, the true Intercessor, etc., etc. Such discussions, though sometimes warm, and from the Moslem side fierce, were not altogether without their uses. They served as a means of popular education upon many of the vital points of difference between Islam and Christianity. They were a means of rendering the Christians more steadfast in their faith. So influential indeed were they, that by and by the mullahs forbade the faithful to listen to such debates or to read books in which the questions were discussed from the Christian standpoint.

The most effective work for Moslem evangelisation, however, has been done through the schools in which the spiritual lessons of the Bible are regularly taught. Here thought is aroused and a spirit of inquiry created. Such young men as have been thus strongly influenced have frequently come out boldly and confessed themselves Christians, and from among these have been raised up many of the most efficient among the native evangelists and pastors in the Indian churches. The open confession of faith often costs a price well nigh as precious as life itself. It means not only the loss of all things, but danger to life itself. Some have forfeited even their lives for the sake of the Gospel. An Afghan mullah was led to Christ, and so earnest was he that he insisted upon preaching to his former co-religionists, notwithstanding the threats made against his life. He said, "The Lord's will be done, but I must preach the Gospel." One night the silence of the darkness was disturbed by a gunshot. The cry of murder was raised, the zealous convert was dead. Sometimes the convert only saves his life by flight. All such confessions serve to strengthen the faith and courage of others.

When Moslems come out and ask for baptism, the most common reason assigned for their change of faith is the reading of the Bible or some religious book or tract. A young Kashmiri was the assistant to an English officer, a devoted Christian, who was hunting wild animals in the mountains of Kashmir. Every night the Moslem youth noticed his master reading a book and then praying to God. He ventured to inquire what book he was reading. The young officer said he was reading the New Testament and explained what some of its teachings were. He then offered to procure a copy in the vernacular, if the Moslem would promise to read it. The promise was given, and by and by the youth sought a missionary and confessed his faith in Christ by baptism. That young man is now an old man, a minister of the Gospel and pastor of a congregation numbering some two hundred souls. Two of his converts were Moslem youths who are now also pastors of churches in the Punjab.

The influence of the missionaries and their converts

in India upon the Moslem population has been sufficient to place the Moslem upon the defensive. Schools for boys, and to some extent for girls, also have been established, so as to provide for the education of their children without exposing them to the influences of the Christian schools. The mosques have been repaired and every effort made to prohibit attendance upon places of Christian worship and the reading of Christian books. Schools for the training of preachers have been established under the auspices of the society for the conservation of Islam. These preachers are trained in the art of debate, and their minds well stocked with the usual objections raised by Moslems against the Bible and the Christian teachings concerning the Trinity, the divinity of Christ, and salvation by atonement. Tracts are provided inveighing against Christianity and the work of the missionaries. Armed with these, the Moslem preachers go forth, and by methods not unlike those of the missionaries and native preachers, they endeavour to win over to Islam the ignorant, low-caste population, and even to reclaim any who have lapsed and become members of a Christian church.

The more highly educated Moslems usually adopt the agnostic and rationalistic arguments of Christian unbelief, and thus strive to supplant the Gospel teaching which intelligent men cannot now avoid. Many of these men do not hesitate to announce themselves as rebels against the teachings of the Moslem fathers, the Imams, and the Mujtahids, but still hold on to the system of the Moslem faith as being superior to Christianity.

One sect has announced its belief that Moslems must

abandon the teaching of the orthodox leaders, that Jesus did not die as other men die, because Islam cannot stand against the belief that Jesus lives and is exalted in glory. To this end they teach that the Jesus of Christianity did not die upon the cross, but merely swooned and was afterward restored to life and escaped. Travelling east into Thibet, he eventually returned to Kashmir, where he died and where his tomb may now be seen. Absurd as this attempt to apply the old swoon theory to the needs of Islam is, it suggests the conscious weakness of Islam in the presence of the historic Christ. "Who is your intercessor?" asks the Christian. "Mohammed," says the Moslem, "is our intercessor. He will intercede for all true believers on the Judgment Day." The Christian replies, showing the need of a present intercessor, and points out the fact that the question of salvation, according to the Quran, is decided on this side the Dark Valley, for does it not say the Judgment Day "is a day whereon one soul shall not be able to obtain anything in behalf of another soul; and the command on that day shall be God's"? The Moslem then asks, "Who then is the present-day intercessor?" to which the Christian replies, "The living and exalted Saviour, Jesus the Christ, who ever liveth to make intercession for us." Why go to the tombs of dead prophets, however holy and exalted they may have been in life? They, too, have need of a Saviour, having been sinful as we are. Go to the Living Intercessor who alone among your prophets is accounted sinless in your Quran and Traditions. And is He not to come again to destroy antichrist, *Dajjal,* and to restore the true faith to the world? Jesus, He is our intercessor. He has triumphed over death and hell. He stands at the right hand of God. He waits to intercede for thee. Come then to Jesus our great intercessor."

In the earlier years of missionary endeavour in India the public preaching of the evangelists aroused the fiercest opposition of the mullahs and maulvies, who came forth with many arguments to expose the errors of the Christians and to maintain the Moslem contention. Of this controversy we shall speak in another place. At the present moment the Christian missionary feels that the effect of controversy is rather to stir up and to crystallise Moslem prejudice. The missionary endeavours to avoid all public debate on religious questions, and studies how he may present the claims of Christ to the Moslem in a sympathetic and tactful way. He depends more upon the silent influence of the Word of God, especially as found in the Gospels and the Psalms. The books and tracts he uses are written in the same sympathetic spirit. This attitude may be said to mark a new era in the work of Moslem evangelisation.

The accessions from Islam, especially in Northern India, have been continuous during all the years since the death of Henry Martyn. One here and another there, has been added to the Christian Church, so that now as one looks over the rolls of church membership, he is surprised to find so many converts from Islam, or the children and children's children of such converts. In the North, especially the Punjab, and the Northwest Frontier Province, every congregation has a representation from the Moslem ranks. Some of the churches have a majority of their membership gathered from amongst the Mussulmans. In a few cases there has been something like a movement among Moslems towards Christianity, and a considerable number have come out at one time. But perhaps the fact which tells most clearly the story of the advance of Christianity among Moslems in India, is this, that among the native pastors and Christian preachers and teachers in North India, there are at least two hundred who were once followers of Islam. Among the names of those who have gone to their reward, many of them after long lives of faithful service, some of my readers will recall the names of the Rev. Maulvie Imaduddin, D. D., Maulvie Safdar Ali, E. A. C., Munshi Mohammed Hanif, Sayyad Abdullah Athim, E. A. C., the Rev. Rajab Ali, Sain Gamu Shah, the Rev. Abdul Masih, the Rev. Ashraf Ali, the Rev. Jáni Ali, and Dilawur Khan. These faithful servants of God have left behind them memories which still live. Many of them have bequeathed volumes of literature, which have added much to the literary wealth of all the churches. They give us an index wherewith to guide us as to what the strength and character of the Church of the future will be when the strong champions of the Crescent shall have become the champions of the Cross.

Recently there was held in Cairo in Egypt a conference of missionaries to canvass the whole question of the evangelisation of the Moslem world.

There were present sixty-two delegated members besides some fifty or sixty visiting members. The whole ground was gone over in the papers read, and the discussions which followed, all of which have since become available for the use of those specially interested. Some points brought out at this conference suggest to all friends of Moslem evangelisation changes and improvement of methods which would greatly increase the efficiency of the work. These suggestions will no doubt lead many workers in India to undertake to carry them out. One lesson learned is that every missionary society carrying on work in Moslem lands, should encourage some of its missionaries to thoroughly master the Arabic language and the literature of Islam, in order better to understand the Moslem people, and to approach them in a more tactful way than is possible to those who are not thus instructed.

Another lesson learned is the need of a great sympathetic heart which will consider the position of the Moslem, and honour him for his manly defence of what he believes to be true. A heart which will acknowledge the truth taught in the Quran and the literature of Islam.

A third lesson for us to learn in India and the Far East is the need of the power of the Holy Spirit to make effective the work already being done. The power and influence of intercessory prayer is being realised now more than ever. There must be a continual reliance upon the Word of God as the agency which will convict men of sin.

Still another point is the need of not only a larger work for the evangelisation of Moslems, but an increased endeavour to gather into the Christian fold the millions of ignorant idolaters who are being rapidly converted to Islam. No work can so strongly commend Christians to the sincere Moslem as this work of destroying idolatry in the earth.

A final step toward the accomplishment of this work is to unify as far as possible the whole literature now being published for Moslem readers. The Church of God must teach one lesson to the Moslems in all lands. Then as far as possible let all denominations of Christians unite to establish in each country one united Church, which shall present an unbroken front to the Moslem world.

In India and China something has been accomplished in this direction. Nine bodies of Presbyterians have united to found one church. Besides this, steps have been taken to bring about, if possible, a union of all evangelical Christians in one Indian Protestant Church. Similar movements have been reported from China. In the Dutch East Indies there is but one church, so that Christianity is there represented by the one church of Holland.

The Protestant Church has thus entered upon its most important work for the world's evangelisation. The opportunity is hers. The Anglo-Saxon races are hers, and they are now directly or indirectly in control of the world's Moslem populations. Much of the wealth and learning of the world are in her hands. The spirit of philanthropy, which bestows religious liberty, education and just treatment in national counsels are hers. To millions of Moslems they have been benefactors, and these in turn have reciprocated by loyal service as officers and citizens and soldiers in the time of need. All this reveals to us the finger of God pointing the way wherein the spiritual descendants of Isaac and Ishmael may meet upon the common ground of faith in the true God, and the leadership of Him who is now the exalted Saviour of all the children of Abraham.

VI

THE MOSLEM CONTROVERSY[1]

CONTROVERSY between Christians and Moslems in India had its inception in the fertile genius of the Mogul Emperor Akbar the Great. Stanley Lane Poole, describing the wonders of the deserted city of Fathpur-Sikri, which was built by Akbar, as a royal suburb to Agra, his capital, says: "We may stand in the audience hall, with its pillar throne and galleries, where the keenest dialectic of Moslem schoolmen, Catholic priests, Pantheists, Fireworshippers, Brahmans, and Buddhists rose in heated battle for their creeds, till quarrels and coarse vituperation called up the bitter sneer of the puritanic Badauni, and the regretful contempt of the royal seeker after truth."[2] Here it was that Akbar held his Parliament of Religions, and to which he welcomed the representatives of all religions. His historian Badauni tells us something in regard to the coming of these priests to the court of Akbar and of their employment while there. He says:[3]

"In 986 A. H. [1578 A. D.], the missionaries of Europe, who are called Padres, and whose chief Pontiff, called Papa, promulgates his interpretations for the use of the people, and who issues mandates that even kings

[1] For an account of method of controversy see Appendix II.

[2] *Mediaeval India*, p. 272.

[3] *Badauni*, ii, 260, quoted in *Mediaeval India*, p. 273, note.

dare not disobey, brought their Gospel to the emperor's notice, advanced proofs of the Trinity, and affirmed the truth and spread abroad the knowledge of the religion of Jesus. The emperor ordered Prince Murad to learn a few lessons from the Gospel, and to treat it with all due respect, and Sheikh Abul Fazl was ordered to translate it. Instead of the prefatory *Bismillah,* the following ejaculation was enjoined, 'O, thou whose name is Jesus Christ.'"

It was no doubt in consequence of these liberal influences surrounding the court of Akbar and his son, the Emperor Jahangir, that the discussions carried on in the city of Lahore, and which are summed up in Hieronymo Xavier's book *Aina-i-Haqq-Numa,* were possible. Xavier's book is the first written apology for the Christian religion ever addressed to an Indian audience. It was addressed to Moslems and was dedicated to the Emperor Jahangir, the title bearing these words, "Address to the Shadow of God, the Asylum of Empire, the great King of Kings, Jahangir. May God perpetuate his kingdom and power."

An examination of the contents of this book, comprising 800 pages, discloses the fact that the main points of contention between Christian and Moslem, in the capital city of the Punjab three centuries ago were practically the same as those still discussed in the bazaars and chapels of Lahore to-day. These points are: the mystery of the Holy Trinity, the Divinity of the Messiah, the Integrity of the Christian Scriptures and the Moslem claim that the former Scriptures have been abrogated by the Quran. Excepting the portion of this book devoted to the defence of image worship and the reverence bestowed upon relics and saints, the discussions were conducted with considerable ability. On the practical aspects of the teaching of the Quran, the missionary attacked its immoral teaching in respect to marriage, polygamy, divorce, etc., and represented the facility with which Islam ministers to the desires and passions of men, as like unto the production of a cook, who studies the palate of his master, while the less attractive aspects of Christianity are like unto the bitter of a wholesome medicine.

The principal point of interest to us in the examination of this controversy is that the attitude of the Mohammedan world toward Christian belief was already fixed. The fundamental and inexorable antagonism of Islam toward the religion of the Bible was clearly established. For this statement we are fortunately not dependent upon inferences drawn from Hieronymo Xavier's book. A Moslem reply to this book was written twelve years after its appearance (1621 A. D.) and a copy still exists, discovered by Professor S. Lee, D. D., M. R. A. S., in the library of the Cambridge University. It is a volume comprising three hundred and fifty 12mo pages, written by a Persian nobleman named Ahmad Ibn Zain al-Abidin, and bears the somewhat pompous title, *Al Namia ar Rabania Fi Radd ush-Shubahi-n-Nusarani:* "The Divine Rays in refutation of Christian Error."

In this book the writer undertakes to refute the Christian padres by proofs drawn from the Gospel, the Pentateuch and the Psalms. He claims that since

Mohammed is the Paraclete, Christians disobey Christ in rejecting him as the prophet of God, who was sent "to teach men that the Messiah was the Son of Man as it occurs in the Psalms."[4] The passage here alluded to is Ps. ix. 20: "Put them in fear, O Lord; that the nations may know themselves to be but men." This verse is garbled to read thus: "O God, send a lawgiver that he may come and teach men that he [the Messiah] is man," and the writer goes on to say, "Hence it is plain that God informed David of what the Christians would say respecting Christ, after which he is informed that God would send some one who would establish a law, and teach mankind the right way, and that the Messiah would be a man. Hence to worship him is inexcusable, much more to consider him as God!"

We are here reminded of a criticism of this writer by the late Sir William Muir, in which he said: "His direct arguments against Christianity consist chiefly of the usual components of a Mohammedan attack,—groundless reasonings and perverted interpretations of Scripture."[5]

Another verse or two may be given to show how this writer proves the mission of his prophet by reference to the Christian Scriptures. Deut. xxxiii. 2 is cited to prove this claim: "The Lord came from Sinai, and rose up

[4] This passage is characteristic of Moslem reasoning. We have here three unproven assumptions: (1) That Mohammed is a prophet; (2) that Mohammed is the paraclete; and (3) that David foretold that Mohammed would be sent to teach Christians that the Messiah was a man and not divine.

[5] *The Mohammedan Controversy*, p. 8.

from Seir unto them; he shined forth from Mount Paran." In this passage Sinai means Moses, while Seir means Galilee, in a village of which Messiah dwelt. Mount Paran means the Revelation of Mohammed, because Paran is a mountain in the neighbourhood of Mecca in Arabia!

The Prophet Habakkuk iii. 3, is said to refer to Mohammed by name, because the Hebrew word translated "Praise" is the same as Ahmad (meaning Praise). Genesis xvii. 20, in which God gives a promise of blessing to Ishmael, is made to apply to Mohammed. Psalm l. 2, "Out of Zion, the perfection of beauty, God hath shined," is quoted in Hebrew. "Zion" means "Mecca" and "perfection of beauty" should be translated "a desirable crown" (Iklaila Mahmudan), meaning "Mohammed." Thus, this passage becomes a prophecy of Mohammed and his times!

This will suffice for a sample of the way in which the Old Testament Scriptures were perverted and garbled in order to furnish support to Mohammed's prophetic claim. To any one conversant with Moslem controversy, it will be apparent that this method of argument is still adhered to by our Moslem antagonists unless they have become sufficiently enlightened by modern European education to see the absurdity of the attempt.

Further on this writer refers to the so-called contradictions of the Christian Scriptures to prove their corruption. Polygamy is defended by reference to the example of the Patriarchs. The Genealogies of Matthew and Luke come in for the usual comment. The doctrines of the Sonship of Christ and the Trinity are held up to ridicule, and so on in a strain familiar to every missionary and worker among Mohammedans. Most of the arguments seem to be set forth in all sincerity, but ignorance of the teachings of Scripture added to Moslem prejudice accounts for most of the conclusions arrived at. What the outcome of this controversy was we have no means of learning. It is, however, to be feared the exhortations of the Catholic padres to worship Mary and the saints and their claim that the use of images was right, would rather confirm the Moslems in their errors.

The next stage in the Mohammedan controversy, worthy of special notice, is that which began with the visit of Henry Martyn to the city of Shiraz in Persia. As the result of his public discussions with the Persian mullahs, there soon appeared a pamphlet, in the Persian language, written by Mirza Ibrahim, "the preceptor of all the mullahs," which purported to be a refutation of the teachings of Henry Martyn. It was written in a kindly spirit and was regarded as the most effective book yet written from the Mohammedan standpoint. The booklet was almost wholly devoted to the question of miracles and the establishment of the claim that the Quran itself is the miracle of all miracles. So wonderful is this miracle, that while Mohammed wrought many other wonders, they were almost forgotten in the contemplation of the ever-abiding wonder of the matchless Quran. "This miracle," says Mirza Ibrahim, "will forever remain just what it was at the first propagation of Islam, contrary to the character of the miracles of other prophets, of which we have nothing remaining but mere narratives, as, for instance Moses or Jesus did this or that; or it is thus preserved by tradition. But no narrative can carry with it the evidence of an eye-witness. The miracles of other prophets, moreover, in addition to their want of evidence, as already noticed, when compared with that of the Quran will by length of time become less and less convincing; because in process of time any narrative must become less impressive. But the miracle of the Quran, on the contrary, will, in process of time, become more impressive, because the learned, who have confessed their inability to produce the like, will have been more numerous, though the miracle itself will remain exactly what it was at the first; and the conviction of its being a miracle will thus become more powerful."

This booklet assaults the credibility of the Christian Scriptures and very consistently refrains from quoting them in evidence of the Moslem claims. The teaching of the former Scriptures is to be found in the Quran alone. Mirza Ibrahim sets himself squarely upon the matchless Quran and claims that it alone is sufficient to satisfy any reasonable man. "Judge then," says he, "how any sensible man can leave that which is true, to embrace what is manifestly implicated in doubt."

To this book we have in reply the three tracts of Henry Martyn, translated into English by Professor Lee, and published in his book already quoted. In the first tract he not only proves from the Quran that Mohammed wrought no miracles but shows the impossibility of the Quran itself being a miracle in any true sense of the word, because it could not be generally intelligible. He then goes on to disprove the prophetic claims of Mohammed. In the second tract, he enlarges upon the position of the first and refutes the claim of Islam to be the true religion. In the third he addresses himself to the peculiar doctrines of the Persian Sufis.

These tracts brought forth a lengthy reply by Mohammed Raza of Hamadan, Persia. This work appeared in 1813, the year after Henry Martyn's death. It occupies 289 pages. Sir William Muir describes it as "not being characterised by any peculiar exhibition of talent, and abounding with perversions of Scripture and unfair conclusions, such as we meet with nowadays in India."[6]

A very noticeable characteristic of Mirza Ibrahim's reply is that it reproduces in the main the arguments already noticed in the reply of Ahmad Ibn Zain al-Abidin to the Catholic padre, Hieronymo Xavier of Lahore. It is quite probable that Mirza Ibrahim had access to that book. The absence of any idolatrous teaching in the tracts of Henry Martyn deprived this writer, as well as all who succeeded him, of the opportunity to reproach the Protestant Christian apologist with idolatrous worship. This fact marks a decided advance in the cause of the Christian as against the Moslem antagonist. Islam had at last been confronted by a pure Christianity.

Another point, which should not be overlooked, is the practical admission by Mirza Ibrahim, above mentioned, that Islam cannot afford to recognise the Christian Scriptures as even credible histories, much less as the inspired books attested by the Quran. He writes

[6] *Mohammedan Controversy*, p. 15.

thus: "We say, we are not sure of the miracles of that Moses and Jesus of whom the Jews and Christians speak, and who, as they say, did not believe in the mission of our prophet; but we speak of the miracles of that Moses and Jesus which have given their testimony to the mission of Mohammed: and how great a difference between them when viewed in these different lights! Let it not here be said that the persons are the same in both cases; and that the difference consists merely in the circumstances in which the different accounts have placed them. For we persist in affirming that the circumstance of their not having borne testimony to the mission of Mohammed in the first place, is sufficient to warrant our denial of their identity with the second."[7]

On the other hand, we find that the Mohammedan advocate, Mohammed Raza of Hamadan, recognises the Christian Scriptures as corrupted copies of the Scriptures mentioned in the Quran. Indeed his book is largely made up of a perversion of numerous passages taken from these Scriptures, making them foretell the advent of Mohammed and the triumphs of Islam. Such a course could not but lead to a final recognition of the inspiration of the Scriptures, at least in the Sayyad Ahmad sense.[8]

A very satisfactory discussion of the questions raised by the Henry Martyn controversy is to be found in Dr. Lee's work, which is the concluding section of the Persian controversies. Sir William Muir gives us the following brief outline of the argument in this work:

"In his first chapter he exposes the insufficiency of

[7] Lee's *Persian Controversies*, p. 32.

[8] *Commentary on Genesis* by Sayyad Ahmad Khan.

the evidence upon which Moslems lean, and shows that the testimony of multitudes of interested parties, who were only partially informed, is worth nothing. He then substitutes instead the true laws of evidence as enforced by Locke's six considerations. The second chapter is devoted to the integrity of the Scriptures. . . . This whole chapter is recommended to the particular attention of our missionaries. In his third chapter, Dr. Lee, foregoing the proof by miracles, shows from Scripture that a true prophet must have the gift of prophecy; and that even then, if he opposes a previous revelation, he is not to be credited: Mohammed is condemned by these premises. The argument concludes with a brief description of our Scriptures, in which, avoiding metaphysical and abstruse arguments, he dwells on their adaptation to man, and refutes the objections of the Moslems."[9]

It was at about the time when Dr. Lee published his book on the Persian controversies that the Basel Missionary Society sent out to Persia a man who was destined to advance the assault upon the Moslem works further than any one who had yet appeared in the field. It was some time between 1824 and 1829 that the Rev. C. G. Pfander arrived in Shusha and devoted himself especially to the work of missions among Moslems. After acquiring the Persian language he began to preach in various places in Persia. At Kermanshah he narrowly escaped the crown of martyrdom. It was while yet in Persia that he published his great work, the *Mizan-ul-Haqq,* or the "Balance of Truth," a book which aroused more discussion among Mohammedans

[9] *The Mohammedan Controversy,* p. 17.

than any book of that century. It has been translated into almost every Moslem language of the world. In 1835 the Basel Mission in Shusha and Persia was closed by a royal *Ukase* of the Russian Government. Dr. Pfander came to India and established himself at Agra, where he produced an Urdu edition of the *Mizan-ul-Haqq*. This work and others which he wrote later on and published in the Urdu language have led the way in the Moslem controversy almost ever since. These books, with his public discussions with the maulvies of Agra and elsewhere, so far exhibited the weakness of the Moslem position to the Mohammedan scholars themselves that they were obliged to abandon their own works and endeavour to save the day by a counter assault, in which they scrupled not to use the stock arguments of European infidelity in their effort to overthrow the authority of the Christian Scriptures. This characteristic has marked the Moslem method of controversy ever since. The main points established by Dr. Pfander and his coadjutors in this controversy, beyond all fair dispute are the following:

1. The genuineness and credibility of the Christian Scriptures. In establishing this point, he proved from the Quran itself that the Sacred Books current among Jews and Christians in the days of Mohammed were attested by him as the genuine word of God. He then further proved from the Quran itself and also by other considerations that these Scriptures never were abrogated as Moslems claim. And finally he showed beyond all controversy that the claim that the Scriptures have been corrupted is without foundation.

2. Doctor Pfander, after setting forth in a second chapter the teaching of the Christian Scriptures, proceeded to refute the claim of Mohammed to be the Apostle of God and that the Quran is the word of God. His main points are: (1) the mission of Mohammed as a prophet was not the subject of prophecy; (2) the language and style of the Quran, as claimed by Moslems, afford no sufficient proof that it is the word of God; (3) the contents of the Quran disprove its claim to be the word of God; (4) the character of Mohammed is shown to be antagonistic to his prophetic claim; and (5) the manner in which Islam was propagated in the world disproves its divine character. In his book *Miftah-ul-Asrar,* Dr. Pfander establishes the doctrine of the Divinity of Christ and the Trinity upon the foundation of the Christian Scriptures. He shows the Moslem that as mysteries, belonging to the divine nature, this doctrine must be accepted on the authority of revelation.

Pfander's publication of the *Mizan-ul-Haqq* and the *Miftah-ul-Asrar* called out several champions for Islam. Sir William Muir wrote a lengthy review of the writings of Maulvie Rhamut-ullah, Maulvie Mohammed Kasim Ali and Maulvie Syud Ali Hassan of Agra, and also of Sayyad Mohammed Hadi Mujtahid of Lucknow, who wrote a popular refutation of Christianity entitled *Saulat-uz-Zaigham* or "The Lion's Onset." [10]

The controversy between Dr. Pfander and Rahmat-ullah and Kasim Ali was conducted by correspondence,

[10] *Calcutta Review,* 1845—republished in *The Mohammedan Controversy.* T. and T. Clark, Endiburgh, 1897.

one of the Moslem letters covering 147 pages. The controversy lasted two or three years. These Moslem advocates displayed "the perversity and helpless blindness of the followers of Islam. . . . But Kasim Ali's perversity surpasses that of most of his brethren; he assumes the most fanciful interpretations, and insists that they can be the only correct ones, however absurd and obstinately perverted they may have been proved." In the same spirit the plainest interpretations are constantly ascribed to "Pfander's extraordinary acuteness," and characterised as "phantoms of his imagination. . . . The Mohammedan argument is conducted with some ability and much subtlety; and a surprising number of passages both from the Old and New Testaments are adduced; but the whole is guided by a determined wrongheadedness which adopts the most fallacious and inconclusive reasoning merely because it ends favourably, and refuses to see its errors, however plainly pointed out. This controversy must have proved a severe trial to Pfander's temper; and if flippant contradictions, false insinuations and bitter scoffs may have occasionally led him to make severe remarks,—it is not to be wondered at; on the contrary, we are surprised at the calm and candid manner which he preserved throughout."[11]

To illustrate how trying to the patience it is to carry on such a controversy, I will quote a few lines from Sir William Muir's account of a popular work against Christianity called the *Saulat-uz-Zaigham*, or "Lion's Onslaught": "The chief peculiarities of this treatise are the audacity with which lengthened extracts from

[11] Muir's *Mohammedan Controversy*, pp. 34, 35.

the Bible are, by the facile use of perverse application, turned into predictions of Mohammed. . . . Thus not only is every mention of armies, fear, terror, conquest, goodness or dominion, intended for Mohammed and nobody else, but the Prophet's very horses, swords and arrows were prefigured,—nay his love of perfumes and hatred of garlic and onions were not overlooked. The 'White Stone' of the Revelations must mean the famous stone given by Gabriel to Mohammed, or else it is the Black Stone of the Kaaba, which once was white; and, who could have been predicted to walk in 'white garments,' but our Prophet who was so fond of them! The descendants of Ishmael inherit every promise intended for the Israelites; and more are the children of the *desolate* (*i. e.* Hagar) than of the married wife, *viz.*, Sarah (Isa. iv. 1, etc.)."[12]

We now enter upon a new phase of the controversy with Indian Moslems. Dr. Pfander retired from his missionary work in India and spent his declining years in Constantinople. But the work he had begun was carried on by others and especially by two maulvies who had been converted to Christianity through the public and written discussions just noticed. Maulvie Safdar Ali, lately an Extra Assistant Commissioner in Central India, wrote a very strong apology for his defection from Islam and his acceptance of the Christian religion. This book was entitled *Niaz-Nama.*

Its author rightly perceived that the fundamental question in the Moslem controversy is that of the integrity of the Bible. Accordingly in his book he gave himself almost entirely to that question and also

[12] Muir's *Mohammedan Controversy*, pp. 37, 38.

from Christian sources established the contention that the Scriptures of the Old and New Testaments were clearly attested by the Quran as genuine in the days of Mohammed. He then went on to show that these Scriptures have neither been abrogated nor corrupted. Such being the case, it is clear that the Quran cannot be the word of God because it contradicts the Bible upon many matters of fact, and especially as to the way of salvation. Safdar Ali led the way to a more sympathetic approach to the Moslem hearer and reader.

But the great champion for the Christian faith was the late Maulvie Imaduddin, D. D., of Amritsar, who claimed descent from a royal family of Persia, and whose religious life was much influenced by the addresses and writings of Dr. Pfander. He was baptised in 1866, and ordained in 1868, and devoted his life to preaching and writing upon the Mohammedan controversy. His works number more than a score of volumes, of which twelve are addressed to Moslems, including a Life of Mohammed and an Urdu translation of the Quran. His first work was the *Hidayat ul Muslimin* ("Direction for Moslems"), in which he took up the great work of Maulvie Rahmat Ullah and Dr. Wazir Khan of Agra, entitled *Ijaz-i-Iswi,* in which were gathered together about all the arguments preferred by Moslem writers, such as those already mentioned in the previous part of this paper, augmented by many others gathered from the writings of infidels in Christian lands. In his book, Dr. Imaduddin discusses the question of revelation and inspiration, showing our need of a divine revelation; the condition and signs of a true revelation; the forms and uses of such a revelation; ending the chapter with a discourse on revealed religion, Judaism, Christianity and the claims of Islam. He then takes up the fundamental points of the *Ijaz-i-Iswi,* by which the Moslem writer endeavoured to overthrow the inspiration of the Bible, and discloses the unfounded character of the writer's premises and therefore of his conclusions. From this point he goes on to answer the various objections relating to the charges of interpolation. In this section he turns the enemy's guns upon the Quran, proving that the arguments of his adversary, if true, would discredit the Quran also. Turning now to the positive side, Maulvie Imaduddin sets forth the reasons which prove the genuineness of the Christian Scriptures. In reply to the objections raised against the Bible on the ground of so-called contradictions, various readings, chronology, and morality, categorical answers are given to nearly two hundred objections. Having now established the truth of the Bible, Dr. Imaduddin turned to consider the claims of Mohammed to be a prophet, the sects of Islam, the Quran and how it was composed, and finally the erroneous teachings of Islam. He proved that the language and style of the Quran are not incomparable as claimed by Moslems. The contradictions and interpolations of the Quran were exposed, while the ignorance of the Prophet of Islam, especially his ignorance of the Christian doctrine of the Trinity,[13] and his confounding the Mary of the Gospels with Mary

[13] The Trinity, according to the *Quran,* consists of Allah, Mary, and Jesus. *Quran,* Chap. iv, p. 169.

the sister of Moses and Aaron, clearly proves he was not under the direction of the spirit of inspiration.

In his book *Tahqiq ul Iman* ("An Exposition of the Faith") Dr. Imaduddin set forth by way of comparison the excellence of the Christian Scripture teaching, going into the question of miracles and prophecy. The testimony of history is adduced to show how the Bible has always ministered to the spiritual needs of mankind. He especially emphasised the purity of Bible truth and how it enters into the hearts of evil men, transforming them into pure, humble and holy characters. After pointing out how the Quran fails thus to influence men for good, he ends his book with a solemn exhortation to his Moslem friends to accept the Gospel of Jesus Christ. Doctor Imaduddin lived to see the day when intelligent Moslem writers practically abandoned most of the arguments and objections against Christianity which he and others have so ably refuted.

But this redoubtable defender of the Christian faith was not satisfied to have put to silence the mullahs and maulvies who had been the champions of orthodox Mohammedanism. He had given close attention to the rise of the "New Islam" of the Sayyad-Ahmadies, more commonly called "*Nacharies.*" The late Sir Sayyad Ahmad Khan, K. C. I. E., early in life distinguished himself by openly abandoning the claim of the orthodox party, that the Scriptures of the Old and New Testaments had been corrupted or that they were not genuine. He even went so far as to write a commentary on a portion of the Christian Scriptures. His position was not unlike that of the Unitarians, or of the founder of the Brahmo Samaj. He denied the possibility of all miracles, whether of the Gospels or of the Quran. He nevertheless confessed his faith in both, and taught that a rational consideration of the Quran would reconcile its teachings with that of the Old and New Testaments, if rightly interpreted. When we consider the extent of this movement among educated Mohammedans, we cannot but be encouraged to believe that the impact of Christianity upon Islam has made a deep impression upon the Moslem community. One point is especially to be noted. Orthodox Islam prohibits the exercise of reason in the discussion of the tenets of their own religion. Everything is established upon the authority of the pillars of the faith. Reason is bound and gagged. But strangely inconsistent with this doctrine has been the practice of Moslem writers, when dealing with the doctrines of the Bible. Here reason is let loose and allowed to run unchecked and unguided by bit or bridle. Reason is not only used but abused by being practically made the supreme judge in all matters of faith. This was, as we have already seen, the frank avowal of Sayyad Ali Hassan. Sayyad Ahmad Khan accepted the postulate and boldly applied it to the Quran and the Traditions as well as to the Bible. Orthodox Islam was horrified and a thousand maulvies pronounced him an infidel and his teaching the beguilement of Satan. As a matter of fact Sir Sayyad Ahmad Khan stands as the great champion of Islam, because he bolstered up the waning faith of a multitude of educated Mohammedans, who could not have long continued loyal to the absurdities of old-fashioned dogma.

Dr. Imaduddin saw in this new movement a new antagonist of the Christian faith and therefore set himself to carefully study and refute its false teaching. His book *Tanqid-ul-Khiyalat* ("A Criticism of Thoughts") deals with this new form of Islam. Four tractates are combined in this volume and discuss the following four subjects: (1) Is the Human Intellect the only Spiritual Guide of Mankind? (2) The Old and New Islam; (3) Prophets and Apostles, True and False; and (4) Revelation and Inspiration. These tractates were written in reply to Sir Sayyad Ahmad's books *Tahzib-ul-Akhlaq* and his commentary on Genesis, in which he had made a strong plea for reason as a sufficient guide in our ethical and religious life. On this point Dr. Imaduddin admits that reason has a large place in all human affairs, but, says he, "Reason cannot teach us anything that is satisfactory as to the origin of the universe. Even when a creator is recognised, reason can tell us little as to the purpose of his creation. No more can reason decide for us the questions as to the souls of men: What they are, whence they came and whither they are to go. Again, reason cannot give a sufficient account of religion and a future life. The most reason can do is to lead us up to a point where we come to realise our need of a more exalted teacher." It is on this line that the need of a divine revelation becomes apparent.

The postulates of Sir Sayyad Ahmad that "There is no faith without reason" and that "The religion of of Islam is a rational faith," are both shown to be, not only misleading, but false in the sense intended. The thing that can be understood cannot afford a ground of faith; for faith reaches into the region of the unseen and believes upon the authority of God.

In reply to the charge that, since the Christian believes on authority, he must ever decide for himself what authority is, and that he is therefore after all dependent upon his own reason, the learned maulvie replies, that if Christian doctrine cannot be accepted upon competent authority, we must conclude that Sir Sayyad's doctrine of reason cannot be relied upon. The tractate closes with an earnest disquisition showing the reasonableness of Christian belief based, as it is, upon a divinely attested revelation. The rationalistic faith of Sir Sayyad Ahmad Khan logically leads to the deification of reason.

In the second tractate, Dr. Imaduddin addresses himself to the New Islam, and shows that the pretension of Sir Sayyad, that the Islam of to-day is not the Islam of the Quran, but that his rationalistic system is, cannot be justified by reference to the facts. He declares that "Sir Sayyad and his followers, unwilling to accept the ever-triumphant faith of the Christian, have proceeded to erect, as it were, a new line of defence—a defence, however, composed of sand. As Christians," said he, "we should rejoice that these men have abandoned the old fortifications and taken refuge in the sandbanks of rationalism. May we not hope that some of them will yet be brought to the truth of the Gospel?" The maulvie then gives a description of the tenets of the New Islam, based upon the watchword *Al Islamo ha-yal Fitrato wal Fitrato ha-yal Islamo.* "Islam is Nature and Nature is Islam," and shows that it is hard to understand how a man holding such a creed can yet regard himself as a Mussulman. This must suffice to indicate the character of this new departure among educated Mohammedans and of the kind of argument used by Dr. Imaduddin to meet it.

Besides supplying a great need by writing a Life of Mohammed in Urdu and a book setting forth the teachings of Islam, Dr. Imaduddin has written an exposure of Mirza Gulam Ahmad, the false Messiah of Qadian. We will not undertake to give an outline of his work here, as the Messiah of Qadian is regarded as an impostor both by Mohammedans and Christians and can hardly be regarded as a real factor in the Mohammedan controversy. In so far as he figures as a champion of Islam his methods and arguments do not differ much from those already noticed.

It must be apparent to our readers that considerable progress has been made in the course of these many years of controversy with Moslems in India. We might mention the names of many other Indian writers, whose works have had a considerable reading by Indian Moslems, but we should have in great measure to repeat the arguments already noticed.[14]

We must, however, make mention of a few men who have rendered most valuable aid in the discussion connected with the Moslem controversy. First among

[14] Those who care to see some account of these Indian writers may consult my review of "Christian Literature," written in Urdu for Moslem readers, entitled, *The Moslem Controversy*, published by the Christian Literature Society, Memorial Hall, Madras, India.

these I would place the name of Sir William Muir, K. C. S. I., LL. D., recently Principal of the Edinburgh University. Although he occupied the highest position in the Civil Service in the Northwestern Provinces in India, and afterwards was a member of the Viceroy's Council, he nevertheless kept in close touch with the Moslem controversy. Besides the admirable articles, which appeared from time to time in the *Calcutta Review,* showing a keen insight into the merits of the questions discussed, and disclosing a personal acquaintance with the literature from the Moslem side, which puts most of us to shame whose calling demands the study of such writings, he wrote an extensive literature on Islam, including a *Life of Mohammed,* the *Rise and Decline of Islam, Annals of the Early Caliphate, The Quran, its Composition and Teaching,* and the *Mohammedan Controversy.* We are also indebted to him for his translations from the Arabic of the following books, *The Apology of Al Kindi,* written in defence of the Christian faith 1,000 years ago; *The Asmar-i-Shirin* or *Sweet First Fruits; The Minar al Haqq* or *Beacon of Truth.* Mention should also be made of that great treasury of knowledge in regard to almost all things Mohammedan, compiled and edited by the Rev. T. P. Hughes, B. D., for twenty years a missionary of the Church Missionary Society at Peshawur. The Rev. Canon Sell of the same Society has given us *The Faith of Islam, Essays on Islam* and *The Historical Development of the Quran.* A further and more detailed list of books valuable to every student of Islam may be consulted in the Appendix.

These writings and many others in the English, French, and German languages have gone into the fundamental question as to the credibility of the Quran and the Moslem Traditions and have so thoroughly shaken the foundations upon which the religion of Islam rests, as to have aroused the most serious inquiry among the Moslems themselves. Mohammedans, who are able to weigh the testimony set before them in these writings, find it quite impossible to accept the teachings of the mullahs and maulvies of the orthodox party. Many of these naturally fall in with the deistic teachings of Sir Sayyad Ahmad Khan. Others, strange to say, identify themselves with Mirza Ghulam Ahmad, who calls himself the Messiah of the twentieth century. A few are inquiring the way of salvation through Jesus Christ.

For these movements in the intellectual world of Islam we thank God. The Moslem world has begun to assert her right to think, and we cannot but believe that, awaking out of the lethargy of centuries, she will yet fairly compare the teaching of Jesus with that of Mohammed. When that day appears, we cannot but believe, that the faith and zeal, so long misplaced by want of knowledge, will be devoted to that sinless One, who is now in Heaven, and sits as the Advocate and Saviour of all who come to God by Him.

VII

MODERN EFFORTS TO REFORM ISLAM IN INDIA AND MALAYSIA

THE first endeavour to remove the corrupt and idolatrous practices current among Indian and Malayan Moslems began with the advent of some of the disciples of Abdul Wahab, the founder of Wahabism in Eastern Arabia a little more than one hundred years ago. Mention has already been made of this movement in Java and Sumatra. The leader of the movement in India was one Sayyad Ahmad of Rae Bareilly in Oudh. The Wahabi sect arrayed itself against the superstitions connected with the tombs and shrines built in honour of saints, Pirs, and Walis. It opposed the luxury and vice growing out of the use of things forbidden by the prophet, wine and tobacco and intoxicating drugs. It strove to restore Islam to its pristine purity. It aroused among its followers something of the fierce fanaticism which characterised Islam in the early years of its history.

In India as in Arabia and Malaysia, the movement aroused the war spirit and soon the sword was unsheathed against corrupt Islam and the idolatry of the Hindus. In 1826 Sayyad Ahmad declared a *Jihad* or religious war against the Sikhs, hoping to unite the frontier tribes of the Northwest border, the Afghans and the Moslems of Central Asia under his banner. "He commenced an insurrection on the Peshawur frontier. A fanatical war of varied successes followed, and lasted for four years; but the Wahabi army was soon reduced in strength, and its disasters culminated in the death of its chief, who was slain by Sher Singh in an engagement at Balakot in Hazarah, May, 1831. The remnant of the Sayyad's army fled across the border and settled in Sattana, where in 1857 their numbers were augmented by mutineers who joined their camp.

They were eventually dispersed by the British Government in the Umbeyla War of 1863, but there are still some three hundred of them residing at Palose on the banks of the Indus."[1]

The effort of the Wahabis to bring about a political reform in the Moslem world was a failure. In Arabia, in India and in Malaysia they were defeated. On this point Sir Wilfred Blunt in his book, *The Future of Islam,* says: "The seed cast by Abdul Wahab has not been entirely without fruit. . . . The spirit of reform has remained. Indeed the present unquiet attitude of expectation in Islam has been its indirect result. Just as in the Lutheran reformation in Europe, though it failed to convert the Christian Church, yet it caused its real reform, so Wahabbism has produced a real desire for reform, if not yet reform itself, in Mohammedanism. Islam is no longer asleep, and were another and a wiser Abdul Wahab to appear, not as a heretic, but in the body of the orthodox sect, he might play the part of Loyola or Borromeo with success."[2]

[1] Hughes' *Dictionary of Islam*, pp. 660-662.
[2] Wilfrid Blunt in the *Future of Islam.*

This movement has aroused a zeal for Islam in all parts of India and in Malaysia, if not in China. Its real centre of influence is Mecca, where pilgrims are taught the duty of reforming their religion. These Hajjis exert a strong influence upon the people and much is being done in schools and *anjumans* as well as in the congresses to reform the faith.

The next great movement for reform was inaugurated by Sir Sayyad Ahmad Khan of Aligarh. Born in 1817 of a family boasting lineal descent from the Arabian Prophet, Sayyad Ahmad early entered the Civil Service of the Indian Government, where he spent a long and an honourable career. Like all intelligent and thoughtful Moslems, he was early impressed with the depressed condition of his co-religionists in India. They were apathetic, arrayed against the education which was so rapidly advancing Hindus and Parsis in social and political life, and apparently satisfied to await the will of Allah or the appearing of the Mahdi. Sayyad Ahmad saw the remedy for his co-religionists in a liberal education and an adaptation of themselves to the new environment of a Christian government. He started a Journal, the *Tahzib-ul-Akhlaq* or "Reform of Morals," and promulgated his ideas through this channel. He told his readers that God would help them only when they would help themselves. He was persistent in urging the cause of education and in 1878 he succeeded in getting the aid of the Government to establish a college for Mohammedans which should be conducted as an aided institution. This is now known as the Anglo-Mohammedan College at Aligarh. In all his efforts to benefit the Moslem community, Sayyad Ahmad was opposed by a conservative priesthood. His readiness to loyally serve a Christian government, his promotion of English education among Moslems and his liberal attitude towards the Christian faith, acknowledging that the Christian Scriptures were the same as those in the hands of Christians in the days of Mohammed,—all this aroused against him a storm of opposition. It also made it more than ever clear to the reformer that if Moslems were to make real progress they must get away from the narrowness of orthodoxy: they must accept a more progressive and liberal attitude towards many things. Dr. H. U. Weitbrecht in a recent address before the Church Congress at Weymouth, England, puts it thus: "In some respects Sayyad Ahmad resembles the ancient rationalists of Islam; indeed his remarks on the divine attributes and their relation to the divine nature remind one not a little of the Mutazilite School, and like them he puts forth a modified theory of inspiration; not every part of a sacred book must be equally inspired, we may acknowledge in it a human element as well as a divine. But his thought (system we cannot call it) is more influenced by the conceptions of conscience and nature. Conscience, he says, is the condition of man's character which results from training and reflection. It may be rightly called his true guide and his real prophet. Still, it is liable to mutability, and needs to be corrected from time to time by historic prophets. To test a prophet we must compare the principles of his teaching with the laws of nature. If it agrees with these we are to accept it, and he quotes with approval the remark of a French writer that Islam, which lays no claim to miraculous powers on the part of its founder, is the truly rationalistic religion. Mohammed, he claims, set forth the Divine Trinity with the greatest possible clearness and simplicity: first, Unity of Essence, which he promulgated afresh; second, Unity of Attributes, which the Christians had wrongly hypostatised in their doctrine of the Trinity; third, Unity of Worship in the universal and uniform rendering of that devotion which is due to God alone, thus securing the doctrine of the Unity against all practical encroachments through corrupt observances." Out of this movement, we have had apologies for Islam and the Arabian prophet in the *Essays on Islam* by Sir Sayyad Ahmad Khan, which undertakes to stay the influence of Sir William Muir's *Life of Mohamet,*—also a *Life of Muhammad* by Justice Amir Ali, a judge in the Calcutta High Court.

Another book has been written by Maulvie Chiragh Ali of Hyderabad, which endeavours to vindicate the progressive powers inherent in the Moslem theory of state. Many have written articles in the magazines to prove that the Quran does not inculcate doctrines justifying slavery, polygamy, *jihad* or crusade and the seclusion of women. At the Moslem congress recently held in Bombay the question of female education and the abolition of the seclusion of women was discussed by Agha Khan, one of the leading Moslems of the city. A few liberal men of influence have broken over the barriers raised by the Quran and openly ride in carriages with their wives as do Europeans. All classes, men and women, are rapidly adopting European dress. Some of them send their sons and daughters to be educated in Christian schools and colleges and willingly consent to their taking part in the usual prayer services.

The influence of Sir Sayyad Ahmad has permeated not only the great mass of English-educated men, but through the vernacular organs of the sect a multitude of the more progressive young men have assumed a more liberal attitude towards the social and national questions affecting Moslem interests. Some authorities, however, declare that a reaction has set in against the rationalism of Sir Sayyad Ahmad and that the trend is back towards the orthodox position.

Another reform movement in India is that of Mirza Ghulam Ahmad of the village of Qadian in the Punjab. He claims to be the Messiah of the twentieth century, a Messiah in the sense that John the Baptist came in the spirit and power of Elijah. His business is to teach the true faith of Islam to all men, and especially to overthrow the Christian religion. He publishes a monthly magazine in English and Urdu, which he scatters widely. His followers profess to have witnessed many miracles worked by him and to have heard many prophecies which attest his character as a prophet and Messiah.

He has gathered about him many educated men, some of them graduates of English Universities. He styles his sect as that of the Ahmadiyyah. In his Review he defines the object and aim of his sect as follows: "The chief object of this propaganda is to show to the seekers after truth the path, by walking in which they may be released from the bonds of sin, and taste the bliss of paradise in this very life, and for the obtainment of which Almighty God raised his prophets among all people, and in all ages. But as for the spread of truth, it is necessary to remove errors first; therefore, Almighty God has raised in this age a man whose very claim involves an abolition of the chief religious errors of the time.

"Errors have more or less found their way into every religious system of the world, but in none do we witness a greater perversion of truth than in the system which is named after the prophet of Nazareth. The followers of this religion have given up the simple and noble doctrine of the Unity of God, for a false and mysterious Trinity, and to support this one falsehood they are obliged to give currency to a number of other false doctrines. Every prophet of God taught that salvation could not be obtained unless a man did deeds of righteousness, and shunned and hated evil, but the Christian religion teaches that salvation is brought to a man by professing a belief in the doctrine of atonement, though he may be immersed ever so deep in sins. All these erroneous doctrines are based on the theory that Jesus died on the cross, rose again, and was taken up into heaven, whence he would return in the latter days. The Christians have even gone the length of denying that Almighty God sent His messengers among all people, to point out the true way to salvation, and hold that prophets were raised only among a chosen race to prepare that people for receiving the doctrine of atonement. This error strikes at the root of true religion and righteousness, and hence Almighty God has sent a messenger as the promised Messiah, whose advent undermines the basis of the Christian doctrines. The assertion that the promised Messiah is a person different from Jesus Christ contains a denial that Jesus is alive, or that he was raised to life after death. Hence arises the first principal point of controversy with the two great religious bodies of the world, the Mohammedans and the Christians. That the Christian should have opposed him in this controversy was only natural, because the death of Jesus meant the utter destruction of their religion, but how this point affected the Mohammedans unfavourably, is what I do not understand. Among the forces that oppose the spread and progress of Islam, none is so great as the Christian religion, and if facts are proved, which deal a death-blow to that religion, the Moslems should only rejoice at the circumstance. No principle of their faith requires them to believe that Jesus is alive, and the holy Quran says in plain words that he died. Ahmad's claim to promised Messiahship, therefore, strikes at the root of the greatest religious error of the time, the error that Christ was God, and that he died on the cross and rose from the dead. Hence it is that in the *Sahih Bukhari,* the most authentic work on tradition, it is stated that the advent of the promised Messiah would lead to the breaking of the cross, an expression signifying the overthrow of the Christian religious belief."

So far as Islam is concerned, the special message of the prophet of Qadian is that the Moslem world made a great mistake in interpreting the Quran to teach the duty of religious crusade.

Henceforth the methods of propagandism are to be of a moral and spiritual character. The teaching of the "Messiah of the Twentieth Century," will be so fully attested by miracles as to make it impossible for men to disbelieve!

Under this leader, Christianity need expect no quarter. It must be overthrown or Islam must fall. If Jesus of Nazareth has risen from the dead as Christians claim, then His religion is true. The issue is well expressed and every Christian is ready to meet Islam on this issue. His bold attempt to make Moslems and Christians accept his doctrine of a Christian Messiah as over against a true Messiah, Son of Mary, mentioned in the Quran, suggests the desperation of the Moslem. What shall we do with Jesus? We cannot believe with the Quran that he was caught up to heaven, for that would oblige us to believe in a living exalted Jesus. We cannot believe with the Christians that he died on the cross, because that would necessitate belief in a vicarious death and involve our believing with the Christians the Gospel story of the resurrection of Jesus from the dead. What shall we do? Ah, that swoon theory of Christian heresy will let us out. Jesus did not die on the cross, but was resuscitated and allowed to escape. He travelled eastward, and by and by died at Srinagar Kashmir!

This is the task which Mirza Ghulam Ahmad has set himself. The mass of orthodox Moslems regard him as an impostor, and the general opinion varies between that of regarding the man as insane or as an aspirant to political power.

One regrettable circumstance connected with all these so-called reform movements is that not one of them is marked by any real spiritual life. There is no strong desire to purify the lives of men, no drawing of men to God by the cords of his love, no great conviction of sin. The acme of all reform is zeal for Islam and restoration of its political supremacy.

Another point noticeable is that up to date the Moslem reform movement as well as the orthodox propaganda has done nothing to adjust its system of thought to the environment of the present age. The difficulties which beset the Moslem along this line have been well stated by Dr. Weitbrecht, whose long life among Indian Moslems enables him to speak with authority. He sums up these difficulties under three heads as follows:

"1. In respect of the historic sense. The scholastic age produces chroniclers, but not philosophic historians; in Islam, the truly philosophic historian is yet to seek, especially in the matter of religious origins. Islam has not yet emerged from the scholastic age, and to the Moslem theologian it is the glory of his religion that he possesses a sacred book, every word of which is the very utterance of Allah, come down unaltered through the Prophet and his successors, so that his task is only to interpret the sacred text to the last jot and tittle, *bila kaifa,* without inquiring how it came. And yet he is bound by his religion to believe what explodes his religion. He has no choice but to accept the Old and New

Testament as inspired and true; and to account for historical contradictions between these earlier Scriptures and the Quran, he can only have recourse to a flatly unhistorical theory that the Jewish and Christian Scriptures have been corrupted of malice prepense since the seventh century, A. D. Well may we be thankful that we look for the rule of faith to a Holy Scripture which invites us to prove all things, and which shrinks from no searchlight of historical investigation, so that it come through an undistorted medium; which teaches us to base our faith on facts historically attested.

"2. In respect of the ethical ideal. 'We needs must love the highest when we see it'; and as the eyes of educated Moslems are being opened, they involuntarily substitute Christian ideals for their own. We may and do welcome this as a sign of progress; but it is a practical abandonment of the view which has hitherto regarded Mohammed as the supreme ideal of human excellence. That supremacy was supposed to override ordinary standards; the chosen one of Allah might be allowed to do that which in others would be wrong, and such indulgence was the clearest token of the divine favour. 'No blame attacheth to the Prophet, when God hath given him a permission' (Quran: Sura, xxxiii. 36-38). But now we are told that the polygamous unions contracted by Mohammed were self-denying ordinances for the protection of the widow and the orphan; that the Quran does not really sanction slavery or religious war; and even that it indicates monogamy and the equal rights of women as the true ideal. This is another way of saying that the historical character of the Arabian prophet, far as it might be above the general level of his Arab contemporaries, is a foundation inadequate to bear the weight of a superstructure of universal human conduct. There is only one who fulfilled the Kantian maxim: Act so that the rule of your action may have the force of a universal law. And this universal applicability of the ethical standard of Christ's character and teaching has been secured by a feature to which some have taken exception. Mr. Amir Ali, for instance, regards the teaching of Christ as unpractical, and less adapted to mundane realities than that of Mohammed, who saw that men needed concrete laws and institutions. Christ, indeed, gave the fewest possible directions; he left for the direction of His Church, a life, and the germ principles derived therefrom by His Spirit, and with what result? To take one instance only; the kindly and detailed directions of Mohammed, which regulated and raised the status of the Arabian slave, legalise the institution of slavery to this day in Moslem lands, and lend a religious sanction to the slave trade. But the spirit of the Epistle to Philemon, in the teeth of the most powerful material inducements, broke the fetters of the slave and made the institution of slavery forever impossible in Christendom. The reconciliation of the ethical ideal of man with the thought of modern life can rest on no narrower basis than the historic fact of Christ.

"3. The conception of God. It has been well said, 'There is no charm in the abstract doctrine of the unity of God to elevate humanity. The essential point is the character attributed to this one God.' This applies also to the point we are now considering, the adjustment of religion to modern thought. To reconcile the conception of a personal God with that of an apparently impersonal world process, the divine Being must be conceived both as immanent and as transcendent. Here the Quranic conception fails us. As the ruler of the universe, Allah settles himself firmly upon his celestial throne and thence guides the creation in the plenitude of absolute power, with mercy, justice and wisdom. But with the divine incarnation, the Quran has lost also the conception of the indwelling and informing spirit: in it 'Holy Spirit' is the name of Gabriel, the messenger who travels between Allah on his throne, and the prophet on earth. The notion of the divine immanence is completely in the background, and if in subsequent Moslem theology it comes to the fore, it is always in a pantheistic form. To Mohammed the conception of fatherhood in God connoted the imparting of a sexual element into the divine nature, either as actually in the Arabian nature worship, or by misapprehension in his notion of the Trinity. With a mistaken zeal for truth he spurned the divine fatherhood, and thereby impoverished his faith in its grasp of the fundamental relations between God and the world. The God of the New Testament, from whom all fatherhood in heaven and earth has its name and nature, is above all and through all and in all; in Him, therefore, is contained the full reality of the highest that we know as self-consciousness and self-determination, and equally the fulness of all conscious or unconscious life and motion diffused through every form of natural existence. And for our moral regeneration, this is focussed in the person, incarnation and work of Christ through the Spirit.

"All things are yours: prove all things. The truly historical test leads up to the reality of the absolute moral ideal, which has its basis in the immanent and transcendent reality of the divine Being; and all this for us is realised in Christ, who reconciles the spheres of the moral and the physical world. This message of hope and courage the Christian Church has to offer to the Moslem thinker of our age who would fain find the true adjustment between things new and old."[3]

The hope of those who have been and now are the leaders of the New Islam movement is not in the restoration of the primitive faith and practice of Islam as it was in the early centuries, but in so far as possible, accommodating itself to the Christian religion in ethical and spiritual thought.

It is no doubt in accord with this scheme that the missionary efforts, carried on in England, America, and elsewhere under the leadership of Christian perverts to Islam, have sought to import into Islam as much Christianity as possible. In America, Mohammed Webb boldly vindicated the Quran against the charge of immorality in respect to polygamy, slavery, etc. His teaching is that the Quran does not *oblige* men to be polygamists. Of course it does not. It could not oblige it unless it should succeed in producing the requisite number of wives to go round! But the Quran does justify polygamy, and the example of the Prophet

[3] *Indian Islam and Modern Thought*, by Rev. H. U. Weitbrecht, Ph. D., C. M. S., Lahore.

sanctions it, so that if a Moslem desires to add one or more wives or concubines to the number of inmates in his harem, he is at liberty to do so, and the Quran, the Traditions, and the history of Islam in all ages, will justify him in the act. All Moslems might decide to abandon the practice, but none could quote the Quran as requiring the sacrifice. And so it is that the effort to reform Islam, in respect to polygamy, slavery, the seclusion of women, and the recitation of prayers in the Arabic language, is a concession to the ethical superiority of the Christian faith. It also goes to show that real *reform* means the abandonment of much that is peculiar to orthodox Islam and the adoption of much that is fundamental in Christian ethics.

But this attempt to so far Christianise Islam as to make it acceptable to Americans has proved a failure. The Moslem constituency in India, which had contributed largely toward the Webb propaganda, hearing of his methods, promptly denounced him and sent an Indian sheikh to assume control of the mission.

A similar movement in Liverpool, in England, has been carried on for a long time by a Mr. Quilliam, and some money was contributed towards the movement by Indian Mohammedans. Reports of the marvellous success of the mission were spread abroad. English men and women high and low in the social scale were said to be flocking to the standard of Islam. These reports were denied by English missionaries and declared to be false. Investigation was made and the total number was definitely declared by Moslem witnesses to be twenty-seven. The forms of worship were said to be unlike those of Islam. "'Divine Service,' or *Namaz* [prayer] was attended by men and women indiscriminately, the women not being veiled! The services of a *muezzin* for the regular call to prayer were not available, except when volunteers had spare time! At this so-called 'Divine Service,' conducted by Mohammedans, the prayers which were used were largely borrowed from Christian sources, one such prayer in a Christian setting having direct reference to the Holy Spirit! At the service hymns were sung, and instrumental music used, the hymns being Christian hymns, or mutilated versions of such hymns! Extempore prayer was also used, but little respect to the Quran was shown by Mr. Quilliam himself, and the congregation was moved to laughter by sundry humorous remarks of the preacher, who was also Mr. Quilliam! The service and the performance of *Namaz,* both being in English, was of such a nature as to lead to its being described by two Indian Moslems as *behudaqi* (twaddle) and *besharmi* (shamelessness)."[4]

This Liverpool Moslem mission has undergone a thorough exposure by Dr. H. Martyn Clark, C. M. S., of Amritsar, and James Monro, Esq., C. B., a retired English official who has carried on an independent mission at Ranighat, Bengal, for many years. So clear were the proofs adduced by the latter gentleman to convict Quilliam of practising a fraud that no reply could be made. Even the *Anjuman-i-Islam* of London has denounced Quilliam as "a gigantic fraud which passes by the name of benevolence and religion."

[4] *Moslems in Liverpool,* Part ii, pp. 12, 13, by James Monro, Esq., C. B.

A somewhat similar attempt to improve the worship of Moslems in India was carried on for a while. The principal leader was a European convert to Islam, known as Maulvie Hamid Snow, M. A. U. S. He was picked up by some Mohammedans in the Punjab and for a while paraded as a champion in the bazaars of Lahore and Ludhiana. At the latter place he was imprisoned for two years for attempting to kill a prominent Mohammedan who had been his chief supporter. On his release from prison, he went to Hyderabad and there established an Anti-Christian Society, and for a time wrote tracts, etc., for the Mohammedan Tract and Book Depot at Lahore. One of these will illustrate the kind of prayer and worship inculcated by Maulvie Hamid Snow. Under prayers we have in this ritual: 1. The *Fatiha,* being the first chapter of the Quran; 2. Confession (from the English prayer book) with the following garbled ending: "Spare thou us for we all confess our faults in a penitent and contrite spirit according to Thy promises declared unto the world through 'Ahmad,' Thy Servant, Apostle and Ambassador; and grant, O most merciful and clement Father for his sake that we may hereafter live a godly, righteous, and devoted life to the glory of thy holy name and a pattern to our neighbours—Amen."

Then follow another garbled collect and the Lord's Prayer, a garbled rendering of the ninety-fifth Psalm and so on—everywhere substituting Mohammed for the Lord, and Moslems for the children of Israel. Then follows a responsive service modelled after the English Church ritual, followed by more prayers offered "for

Ahmad's sake." This is followed by a creed somewhat like the Apostles Creed.

The hymns are all garbled from English originals to suit the genius of the Quilliam cult, for the first hymn proves him to be the real author. We find here adaptations of

"Ring the bells of Heaven, etc." Joy for a convert to Islam.

"Oh! think of the Home over there." The Moslem paradise.

"Sweet hour of prayer!"—that "bids us at our Allah's throne," etc.

"Almost persuaded now to believe,
Almost persuaded Ahmad to receive, etc."

"Come every soul by sin oppressed, . . . Believe that Ahmad is the way that leads you unto rest. Trust the Quran without delay, etc.,"

and so on for thirty-one numbers!

It is to the credit of the Moslems that they would have nothing to do with this new-fangled prayer book, and that they closed out this Anti-Christian Society.

We feel that we almost owe an apology for mentioning these attempts of European renegades to inaugurate a sort of mongrel Islam. We have done so for two reasons: first to prove the absolute falsity of all reports concerning the success of these so-called Mohammedan missions to convert the English and Americans to the faith of Islam, and, secondly, to show how closely defined is the issue between Christianity and Islam. Any effort to Christianise Islam is promptly regarded as folly and fraud by all serious-minded Mohammedans. And may we not say that any attempt to Moslemise Christianity would meet with equally prompt repudiation on the part of all true Christians.

It is safe to say that any progress in the New Islam movement which may be toward Christianity, will just as assuredly lead them away from Islam entirely and bring them out into an open acceptance of Jesus Christ as a personal Saviour, as has every attempt to reconcile the Christian faith with that of the Moslem led to a final confession of Islam as the only true religion.

The great value of these various reform movements is that they voice a felt need among Moslems for something better than the best they have. They also help to break up the fallow ground of the Moslem heart, so long bleak and barren of spiritual aspiration. The bonds of creed and custom must burst asunder when once the Moslems set themselves seriously to question their own position, and to allow a fair application of the truths of Scripture and history to the problems of faith and practice. We may, therefore, thank God for the signs of a movement among the dry bones of Islamism, and pray that the Spirit of God may breathe upon them the breath of life and cause them to stand up as a mighty army of our God and His Christ.

VIII

METHODS OF EVANGELISTIC WORK AMONG MOSLEMS

Moslems in India and Malaysia, unlike their co-religionists in Arabia, Turkey, Syria, and Egypt, have but little knowledge of the Arabic language, comparatively few using it except as a sacred classic, and many having no acquaintance with it whatever, except, possibly to repeat a few of the formulæ of the ritual of worship. The same thing is evident when we consider how far the social life of Moslems in India and the Far East has been influenced by its environment. Then the fact of their being no longer subject to Moslem rule has developed among them an independence of thought and action quite unknown in any other part of the world. In addition to this, we should mention the influence of Western education, received through the government and mission schools, not to emphasise overmuch the impact of Protestant Christianity as taught and preached in India and Malaysia during the nineteenth century, resulting in a widespread movement among Moslems for the conservation and propagation of their faith. From all this it is evident that the evangelistic work for Moslems in these countries requires something different in method from that undertaken elsewhere: or, to put it in another form, we may say that methods of missionary work among Moslems in India and Malaysia are possible and even practicable, which could not be adopted among those in other parts of the Mohammedan world.

On the other hand, it stands to reason that any methods practicable in any Moslem community would be useful elsewhere. For instance, the literature prepared by Christian writers for Moslem readers in Syria would be useful among Mohammedans in India. The *Shahadat i Quran*[1] of Sir William Muir, is useful among Moslems anywhere, provided it be translated into a language which they can understand. In like manner, what we shall have to say as to the spirit and temper of the evangelist, the method of his approach and the matter of his address, will have a very direct bearing upon missionary work among Moslems in general.

Let us not here fail to make mention of the vastness of the field for missionary work among the followers of Islam in India. The statistical tables tell us that there are not less than sixty-two millions in India; while the number in the Far East, as we have seen, is not less than fifty millions. This is about one-half the entire following of Mohammed in the world. It is a remarkable providence of God which has placed the largest number of Moslem subjects of any single sovereign under the dominion of India's Emperor. This fact alone should be sufficient to arouse the Christian Church to a sense of her duty to these millions, who profess

[1] The *Testimony of the Quran to the Christian Scriptures*, Christian Literature Society, Madras.

themselves claimants to supremacy in the religious world. Surely the time has come when men, specially qualified for work among these Unitarians, should be set apart for this special work. If there is wisdom in appointing men for special work among Jews, Nestorians, Roman Catholics, Buddhists, or Hindus, there should be no question as to the advisability of preparing and ordaining men for special evangelistic work among Moslems. It is encouraging to see signs of awakening among the Churches of Christendom, and we may now look forward to a day not far distant, when, instead of a few individuals, standing as pickets on the outskirts, there shall be the advance of an army of Christian workers thoroughly prepared for this work and full of the Spirit of the Christ, who is never spoken of in Quran, or Traditions, except as the prophet of love and purity.

Before proceeding to the discussion of methods of evangelistic work among Moslems, let us recall to our minds some of the characteristics of the religion of Islam, which in a measure determine the methods of work among them.

And first among these characteristics of Islam, we would call attention to its teaching as to the Divine Unity. Allah is the only God. He is creator and preserver. He is a personal God, possessing the attributes of infinite, eternal and unchangeable power, justice and mercy. "Praise be to Allah, the Merciful and the Beneficent," is written upon all the outward symbols of Islam. The watchword, "Allah is the only God and Mohammed is the Apostle of Allah," has sounded the death knell to idolatry in every country dominated by Islam. This unitarianism of Islam has been understood in such a sense as to preclude all faith in incarnation of the deity, and especially so as to forbid the recognition of Jesus the Christ as the incarnate Son of God, or the recognition of the Christian doctrine of the Trinity. While it is undoubtedly true that the Trinity against which Mohammed inveighed in the fourth chapter of the Quran (*Surat-un-Nisa*) was a false Trinity, consisting of Allah, Mary, and Jesus, nevertheless the teaching of the passage forbids all faith in a Trinity of any kind. So too, in respect to the idea of incarnation, one passage is equally clear which represents Jesus as confessing in the Day of Judgment, the sin of the Christians in ascribing to him divine Sonship and protesting that he never taught them such a doctrine!

This doctrine of the Divine Unity, which would seem to bring the Moslem so near to the Christian, is, in its Moslem dress, that which makes it so difficult for him either to understand or to accept the claims of the Gospel of Jesus.

Another characteristic of Islam is its doctrine of the Word of God. It is a religion which claims for its foundation a revelation from God through the medium of the angel Gabriel. It recognises the Scriptures of Moses and the prophets of Israel, as well as the Gospel of Jesus to be the word of God. These are frequently mentioned in the Quran, and are always referred to as genuine and authoritative, as the oracles of God. The Jewish opponents of the Arabian prophet are reproached and denounced, because they "misinterpreted" and "perverted" their Scriptures. The modern claim of Moslems that the Christian Scriptures have been corrupted, or that they have been abrogated by the later revelation of the Quran, finds no ground in a fair interpretation of the words of the Quran. The claim of Mohammed was that he was a reformer, a prophet of God, to restore to the world the true faith. This, according to the Quran, was the faith of Adam, of Noah, of Abraham and Ishmael, of all the prophets and of "Jesus the Son of Mary." The Quran, according to this teaching, was an additional revelation from God for the guidance of mankind, and as such, it should have its place at the close of the catalogue of books "sent down" from God, just as the New Testament Scriptures are placed at the end of the Christian's Bible. The teaching of Mohammed as to the mode of divine communication of the Quran to him has led to the Moslem orthodox belief in the eternity of the Quran, securing it not only from any possible error in teaching, but from the possibility of corruption. This naturally leads to the reverence bestowed upon the sacred volume, and the authority of its every word or sentence.

Here, again, we have a doctrine accepted by the great mass of Mohammedans, which is a source of much encouragement, and yet of no little discouragement to the Christian evangelist. Here is a religion, like our own, claiming to be founded upon an inspired revelation, coming from God himself, recognising in theory the Scriptures of the Old and New Testaments, and refusing to believe anything that is not founded on the Word of God. And yet with all this, we soon discover that this revelation is another "Word of God," rejecting and denying the fundamental teachings of the Christian Scriptures. These are, however, conditions which must be carefully considered and which will strongly affect our methods of approach to Moslem hearers or readers with the Gospel message to lost sinners.

Still another characteristic of Islam, which must be remembered by every Christian worker among Moslems, is the *Dignity and Authority claimed for the Prophetic Office.* "Mohammed is the Apostle of God," is a watchword only second to that of "Allah, He is God." Not only is Mohammed "the Prophet of God," the medium by which Allah has made known his will to men, but he is so imbued by the word of God that his every word has become a law to Moslems. Not only so, but every act of the Prophet, yea, every intimation and permission is endowed with inspired authority. Hence the voluminous tomes of sayings and doings, the permissions and the prohibitions of Mohammed, together with the chain of witnesses upon whose testimony the record was made. There is something sublime in the faith and practice of a people not only willing to lay down their lives for their God and His prophet, but who submit themselves in obedience to every word and example of that prophet, as unto divine authority. Such a spirit should not fail to command our respect. Would that the Christian Church were filled more with a spirit of devotion to the Master, obedient to His every word and ever asking, "What would Jesus have me do?" We here learn the importance of maintaining the divine authority of the whole of the teachings of our blessed Lord and of imitating in our lives the example set before us in His life of love and obedience to God, our Father in Heaven.

Once more, we would recall still another characteristic of Islam, which is its teaching that the Way of Life is a way of *Implicit Obedience to God and His Prophets.* A Mussulman is one who submits himself to God. This submission must be absolute. There may be no conditions, no mental reservations. God's will is absolute. Those who have departed from this state of submission are infidels and the objects of divine wrath. Those who submit themselves become the objects of divine approval and the recipients of his favour. God is merciful and beneficent, but only merciful to those who submit themselves to his will.

Now this doctrine of submission, regarded as a statement of the attitude of the human to the divine, is true, and we may truly say that every true Christian is in that sense a Mussulman. "Not my will, but thine be done," is the word of our Lord, and expresses the desire of every Christian believer. But with Moslems, this doctrine has never been understood to mean any more than an absolute submission to the claims of Islam as the true religion of God. Outward and formal recognition of Islam as the true faith of God has always been declared to be the passport to heaven. Very little stress has been laid upon the inner life of the heart. Every form of iniquity, anger, wrath, envy and deceit, impure thoughts and affections, lascivious and lecherous lives, lying, oppression, robbery and murder, when committed upon the persons of idolaters and unbelievers, has so uniformly characterised the Mohammedans as to leave the conviction that the religion of submission is with them a matter of their mental attitude toward God. Obedience is thereby limited to the requirements of the Quran in relation to their conduct. The teaching of the book, and not the dictates of conscience, becomes the sole rule of life.

This characteristic of Islam, however we may interpret the requirements of the teachings of the Quran and the Traditions, makes it clear that *Islam is essentially a Religion of Works.* That many Moslems do interpret the teaching of the Quran in a highly spiritual and ethical sense we all know, but even these are no exception to the rule that *man must do that he may live.* The Christian doctrine, which lies at the bottom of the teaching of Jesus and His apostles, that man must be born again, that the sinner, dead in sin, must be raised from the dead and so receive life before that he can do the will of God, is entirely foreign to the teaching of Mohammed, or of his followers. Here is the contrast: Mohammed says *Do and live:* Christ says, *Live and do.*

This attitude of mind on the part of the Mohammedan world should fill us with profound sympathy. We are reminded of Paul's teaching concerning apostate Judaism, when he declared, "Brethren, my heart's desire and prayer to God for Israel is that they might be saved. For I bear them record, that they have a zeal for God, but not according to knowledge. For they being ignorant of God's righteousness, and going about to establish their own righteousness, have not submitted themselves to the righteousness of God." Like the unbelieving Jew, the Moslem gives a zealous obedience to the requirements of what he believes to be the religion of God, and so strives to establish his own righteousness before God, but fails to see that his own righteousness is but "as filthy rags," and that he needs the righteousness which God alone can give. How our hearts should sorrow for these our brethren according to the flesh, who have so much of God's truth and lack the one thing needful!

We are now in a position to consider some of the methods that should be adopted in order to best impress the minds and hearts of Moslem hearers with the claims of the Gospel. In doing so, however, we do not wish to be understood as intimating that the methods used by many workers in the past and present are open to criticism, or, that we have made any new discoveries in the art of preaching to Moslems. Our hope is to gather up some of the best things we have learned on this subject and present them to others in the way they have impressed us most.

The first point we should discuss under the head of method, is *preaching*. The matter and style of address will of course be determined by the circumstances of time and place, the character and intelligence of the audience, the attitude of the hearers, etc.

In a mixed assembly, it is hardly practicable to enter upon any of the subjects that might in a special manner impress the Moslem mind, or answer the inquiry of such a hearer. The address would naturally be upon some subject of general interest, such as the lost condition of mankind, the destructive character of sin, the compassion of God toward sinful men, or the Gospel plan of salvation. And here we would emphasise the importance of addressing non-Christian men simply as sinful men. We should avoid as far as possible raising what may be called a sectional antagonism, or a party bigotry. Our Lord's example is here, as always, to be considered. He addressed all sections of the Jewish nation, religious and political, but He steadily declined to recognise any of them in his preaching. All alike were in need of reconciliation to God, and to all alike came his words of love and rebuke, of encouragement and hope. Failure to recognise this principle has rendered many a sermon fruitless. A fling at a Moslem practice or belief has sufficed to divert the attention of every Moslem hearer from the main point of discourse, if not to send them away angry with the preacher and his preaching.

We would say, then, that in addressing an audience, care should be taken to avoid expressions that would unnecessarily offend the prejudices of Moslem hearers. Even many of the most sacred formulæ of Christian faith may be wisely withheld. "The sincere milk of the word," is what is best adapted to such hearers. Every effort should be made to bring them to realise the presence of God, and to make them feel guilty before God, so as to raise in their minds the inquiry, "What shall we do to be saved?" Observe that we do not urge the withholding of any truth necessary in order to present the whole counsel of God to the unconverted children of men. We only plead for a careful and thoughtful consideration of the weaknesses and prejudices of the hearer, so that the truth of God, which he needs, may have free course in his heart and he be brought into that state of mind necessary to enable him to appreciate the plan of salvation revealed in the Gospel.

On the other hand, in addressing ourselves to a Moslem audience, respect should be had to the subjects of discourse. Those which are calculated to lead the hearer to a conviction of sin have already been indicated. There are, however, certain subjects peculiarly fitted to awaken inquiry in Moslem minds along lines not altogether foreign to Mohammedan belief. For example, the subject of *the manifestation or self-revelation of God* to men, may be presented in some such form as the following:

1. The necessity of such a revelation that men may know God.

2. The capacity of mankind to know and worship God predicates a revelation of God.

3. The revelation of God in His works.

4. The revelation of God in His providence.

5. Revelation by prophets.

6. The theophanies vouchsafed to Abraham, Moses, etc.

7. The supreme revelation of God in Jesus Christ.

Such a discourse would raise the question of the *Incarnation of God.* This subject being confounded in most Moslem minds with that of *Shirk*, or the ascription of divine honours to any creature, or to any image wrought by the hand of man, we must call attention to the difference of God's act and man's act in this connection. Man may not ascribe to any object the attributes of divinity, nor must he constitute angels or men intercessors with God. We must repudiate idolatry in every form, but that is quite a different thing from God's act, when He chooses to manifest Himself in any manner whatsoever consonant with His nature. Surely no one will venture to question His power to do so. We may then go on to give at least two instances in which the Quran itself attests such a manifestation of God: the Burning Bush and the Shekinah in the Tabernacle. In both instances there was a miraculous light, and the presence of a visible something out of which came the voice of God. Moses bowed before the Burning Bush in worship, knowing God was there speaking with him.

Granting, therefore, any form of manifestation through material substances, we may ask our Moslem hearers, wherein is it unreasonable to accept the teaching of the Christian Scriptures that God was incarnate in Christ in order to accomplish man's redemption?

Another line of argument of a somewhat similar kind may be based upon the orthodox belief of Moslems in the eternity of the Word, by which, of course, they mean the eternity of the Quran. They readily admit that the paper and ink (and even the form of the letters) are of human origin, but the Word thus presented to the eye is eternal, because it is God's word, and God's word and God's thought being inseparable, no beginning may be predicated of either. Thus it appears that the eternal word of God is revealed to man through a material form which is finite. In a sense then, the Quran is an incarnation of the *Kalamullah* (Word of

God), and therefore a somewhat suggestive illustration of the Divine Word of God as incarnate in Jesus the Son of Mary. The invisible Allah is revealed in the eternal word of God; why not in the eternal living Christ incarnate in the Son of Mary?

Another subject of absorbing interest to Moslems is that of Intercession. Notwithstanding the anathemas of the Quran against the heathen who believed in certain angels as being intercessors with God, nevertheless the doctrine of intercession is a part of the faith of Islam. The orthodox belief is that each head of a dispensation will intercede for his faithful followers on the Day of Judgment. Accordingly all Moslems expect to receive the benefit of the intercession of Mohammed in that great day. The Christian preacher has here a splendid opportunity of presenting the claims of Jesus to be the true Intercessor. The fact that He lives and is exalted in Heaven is admitted by all Moslems. We may then direct their attention to His teaching on the subject of His intercession and plead the reasonableness of calling upon a present, living heavenly intercessor rather than wait till after death, when the intercession of all prophets can avail nothing to change the condition of the guilty sinner. The preacher should solemnly insist upon the need of intercession now, while it is the accepted time and the day of salvation.

The writer has frequently illustrated this subject by citing the case of a man under trial for a capital sin. Would such a man go to the graveyard and cry for help to some noted lawyer whose body lay buried there? Would he not surely seek for some one living and in good standing in the court? In like manner the sinner should not hope for help from even the holiest of prophets who lie buried among the dead, but should hope in Him who is alive and at the right hand of God.

Nearly allied to this subject of intercession is that of the sinlessness of Jesus. The teaching of the Quran and the Moslem Traditions are united in teaching the absolute sinlessness of Jesus. They are equally united in testifying to the sinfulness of all other prophets, and especially of Mohammed, who is not only represented as repenting of his sins, but who is distinctly commanded to repent of his sins. This was the subject of the recent lecture delivered in the Rang Mahal at Lahore, by Bishop Lefroy, which excited no little inquiry in many minds among his hearers. The sinless Christ presents a problem which can only be truly solved by recognising Him as the only Intercessor and Saviour of sinful men. Why did the sinless one die? What did he teach in regard to his death? Was it not that through his death the way of life might be opened to a guilty race?

The Resurrection of Jesus affords, perhaps, the most powerful argument for the claim of Jesus to be the Saviour of men. It is the miracle of all miracles. It is the seal of God upon all that Jesus taught. The teaching of the Quran is not consistent upon this subject. There is a passage or two which seem to recognise the resurrection of Jesus; but inasmuch as such an interpretation would involve a contradiction to another passage, which says that Jesus was not crucified, but was carried alive into heaven, the commentators refer these passages to the future, and say that when Jesus comes to earth again, he will die *and be buried in a tomb prepared for him in Medina!* But against all such interpretation of the Quran the preacher can cite the prophecy of the Old Testament and the teaching of the New, and show their accord with all history in regard to this event.

Much more might be said as to the matter of discourse specially suited to Moslems. We must, however, pass on to notice the manner of preaching and even of writing for them. And first we would say, *avoid controversy.* This is, however, easier said than done. Not only is the Moslem ready to debate, but trained disputants and preachers are usually near at hand, who are determined to draw the Christian preacher into a debate on any one of a dozen subjects. The purpose of such men is not to discover truth, but to disturb the work of the preacher, and if possible, to prevent his influencing the minds of the people with the truth of the Gospel. It is a good rule to refuse to debate with these men before the multitude. Let it be understood that an opportunity to discuss such subjects may be had at your own home, but that in your public preaching you will not turn aside to discuss any question whatever. A persistent attitude of this kind will in the end succeed in securing a hearing in comparative quietness.

Controversy can best be conducted through the medium of the press. But even there it should take the form of a dispassionate discussion of the subject in hand, care being taken to preserve a spirit of fairness and frankness, of sympathy and good will toward the reader. This is a lesson not very easy to learn. It is so natural to indulge in invective, and to denounce the sins in the life and character of Mohammed, and to inveigh against the practices and teaching of the Mohammedan doctors and priests. But we are sure that experience will persuade every missionary of the truth of our contention that all such angry debate, whether it be carried on by voice or pen, sadly fails to accomplish the purpose intended, the only result traceable being increased antagonism and bitterness on both sides.

On the other hand, while it is true that the truth of God will arouse antagonism, a sympathetic presentation of it will usually secure a respectful hearing, and at least leave the impression that our hearts are friendly. Where Moslems seem persistent in violent opposition to the Christian preacher, some impression for good may be done by referring to the early days of Mohammed as a preacher in the city of Mecca.

It is exceedingly important to cultivate a grave, dignified bearing. The preacher should guard against all risings of temper. Even a "righteous indignation" may be misunderstood, or at least misinterpreted. Even such small matters as the handling of the sacred volume do not escape the notice of the Moslem. An old maulvie once asked the writer why he laid the Bible on the floor, or stood it by the leg of his chair? He would never hold his Quran below the middle of his waist, never took it in his hands to read without first washing them. "The pure alone should read it," is his motto. It is, therefore, quite shocking to such as he to see the Christian irreverently handle his Holy Bible. Is it not quite possible that we, in our antagonism to Bibliolatry, have gone too far in the opposite direction?

The next mode of missionary endeavour for the evangelisation of Moslems is *the judicious use of literature.* It is often better to persuade a Moslem to read a portion of Scripture, or a book or tract, than to speak to him directly. The advantage of the book is that the message comes to him without the presence of even the writer, and appeals to his mind and conscience in solitude. If written in the right spirit, the book disarms prejudice and arouses conscience. Every preacher should be supplied with tracts and leaflets, and distribute them among such of his hearers as are likely to be profited by them. For this purpose we need a series of tracts, for the most part yet unwritten, which would treat of the fundamental things of religion, and lead all readers to consider those things which belong to God and the highest interests of the souls of men. These should be scattered by millions all over the land.

Many books ought to be brought to the notice of our Moslem neighbours, by our preachers and colporteurs. They should not only be printed in the vernaculars, but also in the English language, as many prefer to read such books in English. The Christian Literature Society for India has taken up the work of preparing and publishing such books and tracts in English and the vernacular as promise most usefulness among Moslems. Among these probably few are better suited than the popular booklets of the Rev. Dr. Rouse, of Calcutta, published in English, Bengali and Hindustani. Dr. Pfander's *Way of Life* is still most suitable for use among the better educated. The writings of Sir William Muir, the *Testimony of the Quran to the Christian Scriptures*, *Sweet First Fruits*, and the *Beacon of Truth* are exceedingly useful.

The question sometimes is asked, "How circulate such books?" It is not easy to secure a sale of such books, and possibly the preacher feels a hesitancy about asking a man to buy a book which is aimed at his religion. The writer sympathises with this feeling. It does seem like an impertinence, if not an insult, to ask a man to buy such a book. A better plan is to send such a book as a present, either by a messenger, or through the postoffice, always accompanying it with a kindly letter, duly signed by the sender. The name of the giver should not as a rule, be written in the book itself. We should shield our friends from the persecution which may be raised against them by bigoted relatives and neighbours. Sometimes it is wise to loan books rather than to sell them or give them away. Where reading rooms are established, it would be well to loan to any who are willing to read. The return of the books will always afford an opportunity for conversation on the subject nearest the heart.

Another way to reach Moslems by means of the press is to circulate newspapers and magazines containing articles of special interest. The new Moslem propaganda, established in Lahore, publishes monthly handbills which are widely circulated by post, or circulated gratuitously at *melas* and other public meetings. In like manner Mirza Ghulam Ahmad sends out his publications broadcast through the mails. A good plan is to secure a good list of names of Moslems, lay and clerical, and occasionally send copies of some of the newest and best publications.

Still another method of impressing the minds of the Moslem community is by a course of lectures by some one who has made such a special study of the subjects discussed as to command a hearing. The effect of such lectures is to call popular attention to the subjects discussed, and secure a widespread interest among the people, even in outlying districts. Here, as in preaching, the lecturer is sure to be beset by the professional or self-constituted champion of Islam, who is ready with his challenge to a public debate. But it is best to ignore him and persistently refuse to meet him, on the ground that no good can come from such debates. The Moslem "champion" has nothing to lose and usually pursues a course of argument which can lead to no satisfactory results. It is wiser to rely upon the truth presented in the lectures themselves, and the power of the Holy Spirit to apply the message to the hearts of some who are secretly inquiring the way of life.

There are those in every Moslem audience who have doubts and misgivings in regard to many things that would be spoken of in almost any lecture. It is, therefore, well to give such men an opportunity to present their inquiries, but they should be presented in writing, and at a time fixed when the lecturer would reply to the questions asked. Such a plan will not only open the way to a most interesting address, but will enable the lecturer to understand better the minds of his hearers.

We will close this chapter by reference to one more

matter of ever increasing interest. Islam in India is on the move. Men of intelligence, and especially those who are educated in modern schools, are no longer able to accept the tenets of the old regime. They are often sceptical in regard to all religions. But there are many who are trying to accommodate the teaching of the Quran to a liberal interpretation of the Bible, and so maintain the prophetic claims of Mohammed. These movements involve the abandonment of some of the positions of the orthodox party. The authority of tradition is discounted largely. Their rationalism leads them to antagonise the claims of the Christian Scriptures upon practically the same grounds as are common to agnostics and unbelievers in Christian lands. The arguments that would influence orthodox Moslems have little influence with these. This fact must not be allowed to discourage us. We must meet this new movement upon other ground. We must insist upon the fact that Christianity is not a philosophy, but a life, and by holding up before them the all-perfect life and teaching of Jesus Christ, endeavour to bring them to acknowledge Him as Lord and Master.

We must believe that, in the providence of God, these millions of Moslems are destined to accomplish some great end in the final establishment of the Kingdom of God. From among them have already come many of our most efficient preachers and workers. Nowhere on earth have missions to Moslems accomplished so much as they have in India. Let us go out in humble trust that by God's grace the Gospel of Jesus Christ will prove to be the power of God unto the salvation of Moslem as well as of others in India.

APPENDIX

APPENDIX I

A LIST OF AUTHORS WHOSE WRITINGS WILL BE HELPFUL TO THE STUDENT OF ISLAM.

AHMAD KHAN (SIR SAYYAD).
1. *Commentary on Genesis.*
2. *Reply to Hunter's Indian Mussalmans.*
3. *Essays on the Life of Muhammad.*

AMIR ALI (HON. SAYYAD).
1. *Life of Muhammad.*
2. *Personal Law of Muhammadans.*

ALI (MAULVIE CHIRAGH).
Reforms in Muhammadan States.

ALI (MIR HASSAN).
Observations of the Mussalmans of India.

ANDERSON (JOHN).
Chinese Muhammadans.

ARNOLD (T. W.).
The Preaching of Islam.

ARNOLD (JOHN MUEHLEISEN, D. D.).
Islam, Its History, Character and Relation to Christianity.

BURCKHARDT, (J. L.).
1. *Travels in Arabia.*
2. *Notes on Bedouins and Wahabis.*

BAILLIE (N. B. E.).
Digest of Muhammadan Law.

BEGUM OF BHOPAL.
Pilgrimage to Mecca.

BELLEW (H. W.).
The Races of Afghanistan.

BLUNT (W. S.).
The Future of Islam.

BLYDEN (E. W.).

Christianity, Islam and the Negro Race.

BRETSCHNEIDER, (E.).

1. *Mediaeval Researches from Eastern Asiatic Sources.*
2. *On the Knowledge Possessed by the Ancient Chinese of the Arabs and Arabian Colonies.*

BURTON (CAPTAIN).

Pilgrimage to Mecca.

BRIGGS (JOHN).

History of the Rise of Muhammadan Power in India—a translation of Firishtah.

CRAWFURD (JOHN).

1. *Descriptive Dictionary of Indian Islands, etc.*
2. *History of the Indian Archipelago.*

DALRYMPLE (A.).

Essay toward an account of Sulu.

ELLIOTT (SIR H. M.).

The History of India as Told by Its Own Historians.

FIRISHTAH.

History of Muhammadan Conquest of India. (See BRIGGS).

FLÜGEL.

Concordance of the Quran (To the Arabic text).

FORREST (T.).

A Voyage to New Guinea and the Moluccas.

GEIGER (RABBI ABRAHAM).

Judaism and Islam, English translation by Lady Macworth Young.

HAMILTON (C.).

The Hidayah, translated into English.

HUNTER (W. W.).

Our Indian Mussalmans.

HUGHES (REV. T. P., B. D.).

1. *Dictionary of Islam.*
2. *Notes on Islam.*

HARDWICK (REV. C.).

Christ and other Masters.

HADJI KHAN.

With the Pilgrims to Mecca.

HOLLIDAY (MISS G. Y.).
Islam and Christianity.
IBBETSON (SIR DENZIL).
The Mussalmans of the Panjab. (In *Indian Evangelical Review*, Vol. X.)
JESSUP (REV. H. H., D. D.).
The Mohammedan Missionary Problem.
KOELE (DR.).
Muhammad and Muhammadanism.
LEE (PROFESSOR S. M., R. A. S., Cambridge).
Persian Controversies.
LANE (E. W.).
1. *Selections from the Koran.*
2. *Manners and Customs of Modern Egyptians.*
3. *Arabian Nights Entertainment with Notes.*
LAKE (J. J.).
Islam: Its Origin, Genius and Mission.
LOW (COLONEL JAMES).
A translation of the Keddah Annals.
MISHKAT.
Translated by Matthews.
MOEHLER (DR. J. A.).
Relation of Islam to the Gospel, translated by I. P. Menge.
MUIR (SIR WILLIAM, LL. D.).
1. *Life of Mohamet.*
2. *Testimony borne by the Koran.*
3. *Annals of the Early Caliphate.*
4. *The Mameluke Dynasty of Egypt.*
5. *The Muhammadan Controversy.*
6. *Translation of Apology of Al Kindi.*
7. *Sources of Islam, translation.*
MARSDEN (WILLIAM).
History of Sumatra.
MCNAIR (F).
Perak and the Malays.
MOORE (I. H.).
Notices of the Indian Archipelago.
MIZAN-UL-HAQQ.
(*Balance of Truth*), *translated from Pfander.*

NOELDEKE (TH.).
Geschichte des Qorans.

NEWBOLD (T. T.).
British Settlements in the Straits of Malacca.

OSBORN (R. D.).
1. *Islam under the Arabs.*
2. *Islam under the Caliphs of Baghdad.*

PELLY (SIR LEWIS).
The Miracle Play of Hassan and Hussain.

PFANDER (REV. C. G.).
The Mizan-ul-Haqq.

PALGRAVE (W. GIFFORD).
Central and Eastern Arabia.

RODWELL (REV. J. M.).
The Koran, translated (and Chapters arranged in Chronological Order).

SPRENGIR (DR. A.).
Life of Mohammed.

SMITH (R. BOSWORTH).
Muhammad and Muhammadism.

SELL (REV. E. B., D. M. R. A. S.).
1. *The Faith of Islam.*
2. *Historical Development of the Quran.*
3. *Essays on Islam.*
4. *Islam: Its Rise and Progress.*

SALE (GEORGE).
The Koran, with Preliminary Discourses and Notes.

TISDALL (REV. ST. CLAIR).
1. *The Religion of the Crescent.*
2. *The Sources of Islam (translated from the Persian by Sir W. Muir.*
3. *Muhammadan Objections Answered.*

WHERRY (REV. E. M., D. D.).
1. *Comprehensive Commentary on the Quran, 4 Vols. Trübner's Oriental Series.*
2. *The Muslim Controversy.*

WISE (JAMES).
The Muhammadans of Eastern Bengal.

YULE (H).

1. *The Book of Marco Polo, etc., translation and notes.*
2. *Cathay and the Way Thither.*

ZWEMER (REV. S. M., D. D., F. R. G. S.).

1. *Arabia the Cradle of Islam.*
2. *Moslem Doctrine of God.*
3. *Raymund Lull.*

APPENDIX II

CONTROVERSY WITH MOSLEMS; ITS PLACE AND METHOD

CONTROVERSY may be defined as intellectual warfare. It may arise in consequence of the struggle of two or more aggressive forces, each striving for the supremacy. It may be due to the desire of one party to supplant another, so that the warfare on one part becomes purely defensive. But whether offensive or defensive, the intellectual struggle is real. It is a warfare.

Religious controversy adds to the forces involved moral and spiritual elements, and for this reason the *odium theologicum* is the fiercest of all hatreds. The soil of this earth has often been made red with the blood of opposing armies, who, having dropped the intellectual armour, have sought to decide the conflict by resort to sword and shield. The words of Him, whose advent was heralded by songs of "Peace on Earth and Good Will to Men," have a thousand times been proved true when He declared that He had not come to bring peace on earth, but a sword. It was impossible to establish the truth of God in the earth without arousing the fierce antagonism of the powers of evil and falsehood. On the other hand the antagonism of the Gospel message is so radical as to make it impossible for the error to live at peace with it. For this reason the conflict between the truth of God and the errors of the powers of darkness is ever a deadly conflict. Like the children of Israel, who were commanded to smite to the death every living soul in Canaan, so the children of God are sent forth with a message of mercy, which is to be carried to every creature—the intent being nothing short of the conversion of all men to the faith of Jesus.

It will therefore, be easy to understand the uncompromising character of the Christian faith. It follows as a natural consequence that the enmity of the world is aroused wherever the Gospel is preached, and its intensity is ever in proportion to the faithfulness with which it is proclaimed or the intelligence with which it is heard.

Is it too much to say that controversy is unavoidable in the propagation of the Gospel? There are those who advocate a policy of non-aggressiveness in missionary endeavour. By these, missionaries are held to be responsible for all sorts of political troubles, and their presence, especially in China and Turkey, is regarded as a continual menace to peace in the lands where they labour.

Now we all deprecate the unwise methods of some who have gone forth as the messengers of the Gospel of Peace, especially of those who have not hesitated to invoke the aid of the State to accomplish their purpose. But we cannot deny that, in the very nature of things, the preaching of the Gospel and the establishment of Christian churches and communities must arouse prejudice and opposition of a very positive character. One of the first signs of this opposition is expressed by the term Religious Controversy. Such controversy is not only carried on by the opposing camps of the Christian and the non-Christian, but is perhaps most commonly seen in the conflict of factions which have arisen within the Church.

In this article, however, the consideration of controversy within the Church has no place. It is our purpose to give our attention to a consideration of the controversy between the missionary and Christian converts on the one hand, and the forces of Mohammedanism on the other.

It goes without saying that the servant of Christ should be a man of peace. He is the messenger of a Gospel of love. He tells of a way of reconciliation with God and of peace with his fellow men.

But on the other hand the whole history of the Church goes to show that nothing so arouses fierce antagonism, as does this Gospel with its doctrine of human depravity and ill desert before a Holy God, its doctrine of salvation by grace as the only way of reconciliation with God. This Gospel is exclusive and can be satisfied with nothing less than the entire overthrow of false religion. We must therefore recognise the fact that controversy with Moslems is absolutely unavoidable.

Some of our readers may be ready to question whether controversy is not an unmixed evil,—possibly a necessary evil, but yet an evil. But reflection will enable us to see that, notwithstanding some serious evils, such as the arousing of prejudice, the possible strengthening of conviction in error, and the creation of a party spirit, yet substantial good may follow controversy. A few of the benefits most commonly observed are the following:

1. *It emphasises the points of difference between the true and the false.* The minds of most men are sluggish and only too willing to be satisfied with present conceptions and ideas, usually received by tradition from the past. If such notions and opinions are false, a war of words may result in a recognition of the error and the apprehension of the truth. If the opinions be true, they become stronger because they have been tried in the fire of thought, and the light of reason. It is thus that the creeds of the Church in respect to even its most mysterious doctrines have been formulated. The intellectual atmosphere is cleared of clouds of misconception and the sunlight of truth is allowed to shine in.

2. *Controversy serves to fix the truth in minds open to doubt.* Speaking of religious controversy, the late Dr. Patterson of Chicago, once said: "I have rarely seen a man converted by controversy. Its chief benefit lies in the influence it has upon those whose opinions are unsettled." As already intimated, this rule operates in both directions. But, inasmuch as truth is more powerful than error, the balance is sure to be on the side of truth.

3. But perhaps the most important result of controversy is *the definite statement of principles involved.* It is probable that the greater part of controversy on religious questions arises from indefinite statements of the truth. Controversy leads to clearness of definition, and thus ministers to definite forms of thought.

4. Still further, it must be said that controversy calls popular attention to the questions under discussion. The incident may occur in some obscure corner of the earth, but

the local interest may extend through the medium of the newspaper, magazine, or the book until it reaches every part of the world. The debate between Dr. Pfander and the maulvies of Agra served to rapidly popularise the Christian claims versus those of Islam. The writings of that great champion of the Christian religion soon became the text-books of every Christian student of Islam in the missionary world, while at the same time they obliged the Moslem world to confront an array of argument against it, such as it had never known before.

Seeing then the necessity and the value of controversy in Christian endeavour to propagate the faith, let us now consider where and when controversy with Moslems may be most profitably held.

This point is not always clear, and the question of where and when we may encourage a debate on religious doctrine or practice is by no means easy to answer, for, however clear may be our theory, we will often find it quite impossible to carry it out in practice. It is well, however, to have a theory, because it will do much to help us in practical work, even if we cannot fully carry it out.

As to *place*, the following general principles may be considered settled, as the result of many years' experience.

1. *Controversy should not be carried on in the open Bazaar.* The circumstances make it impossible to secure a calm and dispassionate consideration of the subject to be discussed. The men who are ever ready to debate in such a place are hardly ever men who seek to know the truth. Their sole object is to annoy the preacher, or to pose as champions of their cult. Oftentimes they turn out to be Moslem preachers, who seek to throw dust in the eyes of the multitude, and so to prevent the lodgment of Christian truth in the minds of the people.

2. *Again, controversy should not be allowed in the course of a chapel service.* Such services should be made as worshipful as possible. The preacher should insist on his right to set before the audience the truth he has come to utter, without any interruption. There are people in every such audience, who have come in as strangers, or possibly as inquirers, and who wish to hear what the Christian has to say.

Any controversy would defeat the object of these inquirers or hearers as well as that of the preacher. Let the chapel service be held sacred to the cause of Christian preaching.

3. *Controversy should not be indulged in during a personal call.* If we have called upon a Moslem friend, it is not courteous to turn his parlour into a hall for debate. If, on the other hand, a non-Christian friend comes to call on us, it is a mistake to permit anything like a hot discussion. A social call should be made to serve the interests of good will and friendship. This is not to say that the subject of religion should be tabooed. By no means, many a time does such a case afford the very best opportunity for religious converse, but that is very different from a debate, which may degenerate into offensive speech which would break asunder the ties of friendship. As to times not suited to controversy, we should say:

(1) *It should not be undertaken when angry passion appears on either side.* The least sign of angry feeling should be the sign to stop. You cannot influence the mind of an angry antagonist, except to make him more angry. If you have given way to anger, you have practically been defeated.

(2) *Care should be taken never to discuss any point, until it has been definitely stated*—otherwise no definite end can be aimed at. In like manner we should refuse to discuss merely trivial questions.

(3) *Debate should be declined whenever the opposition fails to disclose a serious desire to learn or maintain what he believes to be the truth.* There is always hope for the earnest man, but there is no hope of doing good to the mere quibbler or caviller.

(4) *We should decline to discuss subjects in public calculated to arouse angry passion.* The question as to Mohammed's private life or his imposture may be discussed in private, but to undertake this kind of exposure in any public place would possibly, and in some places certainly, incite to violence. Such debates are not unheard of in missionary experience, but I have yet to learn of any good resulting therefrom.

Turning now to the positive side of this question, I would say that:

(a) *Religious discussion may be held in any place and at any time fixed upon by mutual consent.* The discussion may be either in public or private. The place may be the missionary's study, the home of a native friend, the chapel opened for this special purpose, a Moslem place of worship, or in a public hall.

(b) *Such discussion should be on a subject previously announced and clearly defined.*

(c) *Such debate should be undertaken when there is a reasonable hope that it can be conducted in a calm and dispassionate manner.* The object should be the maintenance of the truth against the errors of false religion and philosophy. So much for the time and place in which it is wise to undertake to debate religious questions with non-Christians. Let us now turn to the question of method.

In general two methods of controversy are in vogue: (1) By the voice; and (2) by the pen. If by the voice, it would be carried on, (a) from the platform of the preacher or lecturer, or (b) in a more quiet way, in the way of conversation. If the controversy be carried on by the pen, it would be through the medium of the press, either in newspaper articles, or in books or tractates. In either case, *success depends first of all upon very careful preparation.* The evils resulting from ill-considered debate or discussion of religious questions are very great. It frequently amounts to the confusion of the cause it was intended to aid. The hope of success lies in a thorough study of all sides of the question to be discussed. Every point should be so balustered by argument as to become practically impregnable. In addition to the preparatory work, there are several points which should be considered.

1. *We should invariably preserve a good temper and a serious mood.* The weight and importance of the issue should control the mind and behaviour. The temptation to give way to anger and vindictive speech is sure to present itself. The temptation may take the form of an inclination to indulge in sarcasm and ridicule. But we should not forget that such manifestations of temper are generally understood to indicate a weakening of our cause. Hence we need

to be watchful and strive to maintain a calm and dignified exterior. It is the word calmly spoken that carries conviction.

2. *In public debate, it is all-important to give one's opponent full opportunity to express his views.* It is wise never to interrupt even to correct a misrepresentation. *Take notes.* All misrepresentation will minister to the success of your cause in the end. Complete and respectful silence on your part will enable you to demand a hearing without interruption. We stand up as the champions of truth. This attitude should make us willing to hear all that can be said on the other side.

3. *Be sure of your opponent's position.* If you have taken notes of his statements, repeat them in his hearing and gain his assent to them before replying. It is exceedingly easy, and very common in practice, for an opponent to try to escape from the conclusion of your argument by denying your main premise. If he does not entirely repudiate the statement, he will endeavour to so modify it as to render innocuous what you may have said.

4. *In religious controversy, argument should, as far as possible, be based upon the Bible and the books which our opponents regard as sacred or authoritative.* Reason, philosophy and science may aid you, but in dealing with Moslems, we should pin them down to what they regard as inspired Scripture. The facts of history and religious experience may be used with effect, provided your hearers have any knowledge of either. Everything in their sacred books should be used that is available. For this we have an example in Paul's discourse at Athens, when he quoted the writings of a heathen poet, who had said: "In him we live and move and have our being." A modern example of the value of this sort of help is found in a book, translated from the Arabic by Sir William Muir, entitled, *The Torch of Guidance to the Mystery of Redemption,* wherein the writer builds a powerful argument for salvation by grace through atonement upon a single sentence taken from the Quran: that sentence is, "And we ransomed him by a noble victim." Similarly we would refer you for example to the *Tracts for Moslems,* by Dr. G. H. Rouse, in which we find the Scriptural

teachings of the Christian writer, strengthened by frequent reference to the statements of the Quran.

5. *Be fair to your opponent.* By this statement we do not mean to repeat what we have already said as to giving an opponent a patient hearing. But we do mean that we should never insist upon ascribing to our antagonist a position which he repudiates, or of putting upon his words a meaning he did not intend. Everything of this kind will in the long run defeat its own purpose. It is said of the late Maulvie Safdar Ali, who served the church so long as an honoured member and powerful writer, that when the Delhi and Agra maulvies were boasting that they had defeated the padres, Pfander and French, he said: "No, you did not defeat them, nor did you answer one single argument. You only succeeded in throwing dust into the eyes of ignorant people."

6. *Hold fast to the main issue.* Let less important matters go unheeded, but stick to the one subject in hand. It is a favourite method with non-Christians, and especially with Moslems, to either change the issue by modification, or to raise, if possible, an entirely new issue. You may press them hard as to the testimony of the Quran to the dignity and character of Jesus Christ. They will watch for an opportunity to turn you aside by the trite saying, "Ah, but God cannot have a son." They are faithful followers of the precept, "When ye are persecuted in one city flee to another." Do not allow such change of issue, but insist upon settling one thing at a time.

7. *Avoid any appearance of joy or exultation over the defeat or perplexity of an adversary.* Strive to lead him to see and to accept your position. This is to give him credit with being as sincere a lover of truth as you are. A contrary course is almost sure to rob you of all the spoils of victory. Controversy of such kind as is conducted in a spirit of intellectual pride can accomplish no possible good. Whereas, a discussion, or debate, conducted in humility, cannot fail to impress many minds favourably, and by God's blessing, it may be used to the conversion of some. When controversy is carried on through the medium of the press, the general principles already mentioned will apply. There are, however, a few points that require separate mention.

(1) *Let all matters be presented in a discursory manner.* The danger of the average writer is that he will destroy the influence of his writing by assuming a dogmatic style. Dogmatism in controversy repels. If, on the other hand, we discuss all sides of the question at issue, stating as strongly as possible the positions claimed by our opponent, meeting by anticipation of his argument, we not only secure a better hearing—or rather reading—but we forestall any charge of unfairness or one-sidedness in argument. Every advance in argument should be made in a scholarly manner, demolishing the enemy's defences as we go, and building upon their ruins the edifice of Christian truth.

A splendid illustration of this principle may be found in Dr. Pfander's *Way of Life*, Sir William Muir's *Testimony of the Quran to the Christian Scriptures*, and Mr. Sell's *Historical Development of the Quran.*

(2) *A controversial writer should be respectful in language and address.* By this we do not merely mean that he should avoid giving offence by indulging in sarcastic and caustic language, but that he should use those respectful forms of speech which are invariably used by Indian writers. The bald forms of speech used by Europeans are often offensive to native readers. They not only are not attractive, but they are repellent.

Again, on this point, care should be taken to avoid extravagant statements, especially when they are likely to be offensive. The truth should not be concealed, but it should be couched in language which is devoid of anything offensive beyond the simple statement of fact intended. Quite a large proportion of the books and tracts written on the Moslem controversy need to be thoroughly revised in this respect and some of them should be suppressed.

(3) *The writer of controversial literature should be sympathetic.* The reader should be made to feel that, however much as he may dissent from the teaching of the writer, nevertheless the author is his friend. The reader should especially be impressed with the writer's anxious desire that he should be made an heir of the inheritance of the saints in light. A very good illustration of this spirit is found in Mr. Murray Mitchel's *Letters to Indian Youth*, and

the Rev. J. Vaughan's *What Think Ye of Christ*. The same spirit characterises Dr. Rouse's Series of Tracts for Moslems.

We should never allow the blasphemy of bigoted Moslems to betray us into expressions which could be taken to express mere personal resentment. Patience and long-suffering kindliness will often serve to win an adversary, who would otherwise be confirmed in persistent opposition. Those wonderful words of Paul, recorded in his First Epistle to the Corinthians, ought to constitute the motto of him who would enter the field of religious controversy:

"Charity suffereth long and is kind; charity envieth not; charity, vaunteth not itself, is not puffed up, doth not behave itself unseemly, seeketh not her own, is not easily provoked, thinketh no evil; rejoiceth not in iniquity, but rejoiceth in the truth; beareth all things, believeth all things, hopeth all things, endureth all things."

INDEX